Wampeters
Foma

Granfalloons
(OPINIONS)

A DELTA BOOK
Published by
Dell Publishing Co., Inc.
1 Dag Hammarskjold Plaza
New York, New York 10017

Copyright © 1965, 1966, 1967, 1968, 1969, 1970, 1972, 1973, 1974
by Kurt Vonnegut, Jr.

All rights reserved. No part of this book may be reproduced in
any form or by any means without the prior written permission of
Delacorte Press, excepting brief quotes used in connection with
reviews written specifically for inclusion in a magazine or newspaper.

Delta ® TM 755118, Dell Publishing Co., Inc.
Reprinted by arrangement with Delacorte Press/Seymour Lawrence,
New York, New York
Printed in the United States of America

Second Printing

Acknowledgments

Grateful acknowledgment is made for permission to use the following material:

"Brief Encounters on the Inland Waterway" copyright © Cowles Communications, Inc. 1966. First published in *Venture*.

"Good Missiles, Good Manners, Good Night" © 1969 by The New York Times Company. "Torture and Blubber" © 1971 by The New York Times Company. "Thinking Unthinkable, Speaking Unspeakable" © 1973 by The New York Times Company. Reprinted by permission.

"Reflections on My Own Death" copyright ©1972 by THE ROTARIAN MAGAZINE. Reprinted from THE ROTARIAN MAGAZINE, May 1972.

"Interview" originally appeared in PLAYBOY Magazine, copyright © 1973 by PLAYBOY.

"Fortitude" copyright © 1968 Raymond Wagner Productions, Inc., and Si Litvinoff Productions, Inc.

Acknowledgment is made to the following magazines in whose pages these articles first appeared:

Esquire for "Yes, We Have No Nirvanas"; *Harper's Magazine* for "In a Manner That Must Shame God Himself" and "A Political Disease"; *Horizon* for "Why They Read Hesse"; *Life* for "Hello, Star Vega," "There's a Maniac Out There" and "Oversexed in Indianapolis"; *McCall's* for "The Mysterious Madame Blavatsky" and "Biafra: A People Betrayed"; *The New*

York Times Book Review for "Science Fiction," "Teaching the Unteachable" and "Invite Rita Rait to America!"; *The New York Times Magazine* for "Excelsior! We're Going to the Moon! Excelsior!"; *Playboy* for "Fortitude"; *Proceedings* of the American Academy of Arts and Letters and the National Institute of Arts and Letters for "Address to American Academy of Arts and Letters" (published as "The Happiest Day in the Life of My Father"); *Vogue* for "Address to Graduating Class at Bennington College, 1970" (published as "Up Is Better than Down") and "Address at Rededication of Wheaton College Library, 1973" (published as "America: What's Good").

FOR

Jill

WHO CRONKLED ME

Table
of
Contents

I have traveled extensively in Concord.

—HENRY DAVID THOREAU

Preface

DEAR READER:
The title of this book is composed of three words from my novel *Cat's Cradle*. A *wampeter* is an object around which the lives of many otherwise unrelated people may revolve. The Holy Grail would be a case in point. *Foma* are harmless untruths, intended to comfort simple souls. An example: "Prosperity is just around the corner." A *granfalloon* is a proud and meaningless association of human beings. Taken together, the words form as good an umbrella as any for this collection of some of the reviews and essays I have written, a few of the speeches I have made. Most of my speeches were never written down.

I used to make speeches all the time. I needed the applause. I needed the easy money. And then, while I was doing my regular routine of Hoosier shit-kicking on the stage of the Library of Congress, a circuit breaker in my head snapped out. I had nothing more to say. That was the end of my speaking career. I spoke a few times after that, but I was no longer the glib Philosopher of the Prairies it had once been so easy for me to be.

The proximate cause of my mind's shutting off in Washington was a question from the floor. The middle-aged man who asked it appeared to me to be a recent refugee from Middle Europe. "You are a leader of American young people," he said. "What right do you have to teach them to be so cynical and pessimistic?"

I was not a leader of American young people. I was a writer who should have been home and writing, rather than seeking easy money and applause.

I can name several good American writers who have become wonderful public speakers, who now find it hard to concentrate while they are merely writing. They miss the applause.

I do think, though, that public speaking is almost the only way a poet or a novelist or a playwright can have any political effectiveness in his creative prime. If he tries to put his politics into a work of the imagination, he will foul up his work beyond all recognition.

Among the many queer things about the American economy is this: A writer can get more money for a bungling speech at a bankrupt college than he can get for a short-story masterpiece. What's more, he can sell the speech over and over again, and no one complains.

Preface

People complain so rarely about bad speeches, even speeches costing a thousand dollars and more, that I have wondered if anybody really hears them. And I received an interesting opinion on how people listen to them right before my speech to the American Academy of Arts and Letters and the National Institute of Arts and Letters, which is in this book.

I was seasick with dread before I gave the speech. I was seated between a famous old architect and the president of the Academy. We were three skinny, blank-faced human beings, in full view of the audience. We spoke as convicts in motion pictures do, when planning a break under the eyes of guards.

I told the architect how frightened I was. I expected him to comfort me. But he replied pitilessly, and in a voice the president could hear, that the president had read my speech and detested it.

I asked the president if this was so.

"Yes," he said. "But don't worry about it."

I reminded him that I still had to deliver the detestable speech.

"Nobody is going to listen to what you say," he assured me. "People are seldom interested in the actual content of a speech. They simply want to learn from your tone and gestures and expressions whether or not you are an honest man."

"Thank you," I said.

"I will bring the meeting to order," he said. And he did. And I spoke.

Kurt Vonnegut, Jr.

In this miracle age of organ transplants and other forms of therapeutic vivisection, it would be wrong of me to protest my being dissected while still alive. Two nice young college professors, Jerome Klinkowitz of the University of Northern Iowa, and John Somer of Kansas State Teachers College, are doing just that to me. They have published one seemingly posthumous volume, *The Vonnegut Statement,* a collection of essays about me. And they proposed to do another: a collection of everything I had ever written and which had never been put between hard covers before.

They presented my publisher with an appallingly complete bibliography. I keep no records of my work, and had been delighted to forget a lot of it. Klinkowitz and Somer refreshed my memory with their rap sheet. Their intentions were friendly. They thought of themselves as archaeologists, unearthing primitive artifacts which might help to explain whatever it is I have become. But some of the ugliest artifacts were actually of very recent origin. When I examined all the crap indubitably associated with my body, I did not feel like the ghost of Tutankhamen. I felt like a person who was creepily alive, still, and justly accused of petty crimes.

From all that crap, I have culled this volume. I would not have been able to do it without the help of Klinkowitz and Somer, who knew where almost all the bodies were hidden. There are only three or four works of mine they know nothing about. Not even the ordeal of the *veglia,* said to be the most excruciating torture ever devised by Earthlings, could compel me to reveal where those three or four were published—and when.

This is not a book of my laundry lists, so to speak. I am pleased to have most of this stuff preserved. There are several short stories which have never been collected. I am content to leave them that way, except for one, *Fortitude,* a screenplay for an unproduced short science-fiction film. That is the only fiction in this book.

Everything else in here shows me trying to tell the truth nakedly, without the ornaments of fiction, about this or that. Which brings us to a discussion of the place of the "New Journalism," as opposed to fiction, in the literature of modern times.

Thucydides is the first New Journalist I know anything about. He was a celebrity who put himself at the center of the truths he was trying to tell, and he guessed when he had to, and he thought it worthwhile to be charming and entertaining. He was a good teacher. He did not wish to put his students to sleep with the truth, and he meant to put the truth into strikingly human terms, so his students would remember.

He is to be admired for his usefulness and good citizenship, and so is anybody who writes or teaches that way today. I am crazy about Hunter Thompson, for instance, on that account, and I say so in a review I have included in this book.

Am I a New Journalist? I guess. There's some New Journalism in here—about Biafra, about the Republican Convention of 1972. It's loose and personal.

But I am not tempted to do much more of that sort of stuff. I have wavered some on this, but I am now persuaded again that acknowledged fiction is a much more truthful way of telling the truth than the New Journalism is. Or, to put it another way, the very finest New Journalism is fiction. In either art form, we have an idiosyncratic reporter. The New Journalist isn't free to tell nearly as much as a fiction writer, to *show* as much. There are many places he can't take his reader, whereas the fiction writer can take the reader anywhere, including the planet Jupiter, in case there's something worth seeing there.

In either case, the principal issue, as I learned at the American Academy of Arts and Letters, is whether or not the person who is trying to tell the truth gives the impression of being an honest man.

I am reminded now, as I think about news and fiction, of a demonstration of the difference between noise and melody which I saw and heard in a freshman physics lecture at Cornell University so long ago. (Freshman physics is invariably the most satisfying course offered by any American university.) The professor threw a narrow board, which was about the length of a bayonet, at the wall of the room, which was cinder block. "That's noise," he said.

Then he picked up seven more boards, and he threw them against the wall in rapid succession, as though he were a knife-thrower. The boards in sequence sang the opening notes of "Mary Had a Little Lamb." I was enchanted.

"That's melody," he said.

And fiction is melody, and journalism, new or old, is noise.

Preface

He gave a lecture on equilibrium, too. He stood behind a twenty-foot row of waist-high cabinets in front of the room. He had a string tied to his finger. And, as he said this and that about equilibrium, he appeared to be playing with a yo-yo, which we couldn't see because of the cabinets.

He kept that up for the better part of an hour. At last he raised his arm so we could see what was on the other end of the string. It was a piece of wood molding twenty feet long, with the string tied to its midpoint.

"That," he said, "is equilibrium."

I keep losing and regaining my equilibrium, which is the basic plot of all popular fiction. And I myself am a work of fiction. I remember I was with the theatrical producer Hilly Elkins one time. He had just bought the film rights to *Cat's Cradle,* and I was attempting to become urbane. I made some urbane remarks, and Hilly shook his head, and he said, "No, no, no. No, no. Go for Will Rogers, not for Cary Grant."

I happen to have my equilibrium just now. I received a note from a twelve-year-old this morning. He had read my latest novel, *Breakfast of Champions,* and he said, "Dear Mr. Vonnegut: Please don't commit suicide." God love him. I have told him I am fine.

This book is dedicated to a person who helped me to regain my equilibrium. I say she *cronkled* me. That is another coined word. She came to me with an expressed wish to "chronicle" my wonderful life from day to day on photographic film. What eventuated was much deeper than mere chronicling.

Kurt Vonnegut, Jr.

The *Playboy* Interview with me in this book is almost as fictitious as my fleeting imitation of Cary Grant. It is what I *should* have said, not what I *really* said. *Playboy* showed me a typescript of what I had said into their tape recorder, and it was obvious to me that I had at least one thing in common with Joseph Conrad: English was my second language. Unlike Conrad, I had no first language, so I went to work on the transcript with pen and pencil and scissors and paste, to make it appear that speaking my native tongue and thinking about important matters came very easily to me.

This is what I find most encouraging about the writing trades: They allow mediocre people who are patient and industrious to revise their stupidity, to edit themselves into something like intelligence. They also allow lunatics to seem saner than sane.

Here is my understanding of the Universe and mankind's place in it at the present time:

The seeming curvature of the Universe is an illusion. The Universe is really as straight as a string, except for a loop at either end. The loops are microscopic.

One tip of the string is forever vanishing. Its neighboring loop is forever retreating from extinction. The other end is forever growing. Its neighboring loop is forever pursuing *Genesis.*

In the beginning and in the end was Nothingness. Nothingness implied the possibility of Somethingness. It is impossible to make something from nothing. Therefore, Nothingness could only *imply* Somethingness. That implication is the Universe—as straight as a string, as I've already said, except for a loop at either end.

We are wisps of that implication.

The Universe does not teem with life. It is inhabited at only one point by creatures who can examine it and comment on it. That point is the planet Earth, which is forever at the exact center of the implication, midway between tips.

All the twinkles and glints in the night sky might as well be sparks from a cowboy's campfire, for all the life or wisdom they contain.

As for what happened to some of the people in this book: Not nearly as many Biafrans were butchered by the Nigerians at the end of the war as I had thought would be. The Nigerians were merciful. The brains of many Biafran children are probably damaged permanently by starvation caused by the Nigerians' blockade.

At a minimum, those damaged children, at the exact middle of the Universe, will be more honorable than Richard M. Nixon and more observant than God.

Mr. Nixon himself is a minor character in this book. He is the first President to hate the American people and all they stand for. He believes so vibrantly in his own purity, although he has committed crimes which are hideous, that I am bound to conclude that someone told him when he was very young that all serious crime was sexual, that no one could be a criminal who did not commit adultery or masturbate.

He is a useful man in that he has shown us that our Constitution is a defective document, which makes a childlike assumption that we would never elect a President who disliked us so. So we must amend the Constitution in order that we can more easily eject such a person from office and even put him in jail.

That is my chief Utopian scheme for the moment. My longer-range schemes have to do with providing all Americans with artificial extended families of a thousand members or more. Only when we have overcome loneliness can we begin to share wealth and work more fairly. I honestly believe that we will have those families by-and-by, and I hope they will become international.

I had hoped to include some poetry in this volume, but discovered that I have in all these years written only one poem which deserves to live another minute. This is it:

> *We do,*
> *Doodley do, doodley do, doodley do,*
> *What we must,*
> *Muddily must, muddily must, muddily must;*
> *Muddily do,*
> *Muddily do, muddily do, muddily do,*
> *Until we bust,*
> *Bodily bust, bodily bust, bodily bust.*

One of the lost pieces of mine which I hope Professors Klinkowitz and Somer will never find has to do with my debt to a black cook my family had when I was a child. Her name was Ida Young, and I probably spent more time with her than I spent with anybody—until I got married, of course. She knew the *Bible* by heart, and she found plenty of comfort and wisdom in there. She knew a lot of American history, too—things she and other black people had seen and marveled at, and remembered and still talked about, in Indiana and Illinois and Ohio—and Kentucky and Tennessee. She would read to me, too, from an anthology of sentimental poetry about love which would not die, about faithful dogs and humble cottages where happiness was, about people growing old, about visits to cemeteries, about babies who died. I remember the name of the book, and wish I had a copy, since it has so much to do with what I am.

The name of the book was *More Heart Throbs;* and it was an easy jump from that to *The Spoon River Anthology,* by Edgar Lee Masters, to *Main Street,* by Sinclair Lewis, to *U.S.A.,* by John Dos Passos, to my thinking now. There is an almost intolerable sentimentality beneath everything I write. British critics complain about it. And Robert Scholes, the American critic, once said I put bitter coatings on sugar pills.

It's too late to change now. At least I am aware of my origins—in a big, brick dreamhouse designed by my architect father, where nobody was home for long periods of time, except for me and Ida Young.

There is a piece in this book about Tony Costa, a Cape Codder who was a friend of my daughter Edith. He was accused of several murders. It was decided that he was insane, and thus beyond ordinary punishment. I have heard from him. He cannot believe that a decent, sensible person like himself could possibly have done the killing the police thought he had done.

As his trial approached, incidentally, he was the most famous American then accused of mass murder. At least two books were being written about him by big-time crime reporters.

And then, on the other shore of the continent, Charles

Manson and some members of his artificial extended family were arrested for murdering celebrities. Costa himself ceased to be a celebrity—became overnight what he had been in the beginning, a nobody, a mere wisp of an implication.

That is what I am, too. That is what my parents were. Wisps of implications reproduce. I myself have fathered three wisps, and have adopted three more. It is all so *spooky*. On top of that, I honestly believe I am tripping through time. Tomorrow I will be three years old again. The day after that I will be sixty-three.

This book may stabilize my perceptions somewhat. It is, after all, a sort of map of places I've supposedly been and things I've supposedly thought during a period of about twenty years. I have arranged these clues in supposedly chronological order. If time is the straight and uniform string of beads most people think it is, and if I have matured gracefully, then the second half of this book should be better than the first half.

This is not the case. I find scant evidence in my nonfiction that I have matured at all. I cannot find a single idea I hadn't swiped from somebody else and enunciated plonkingly by the time I reached the seventh grade.

My adventures in the writing of fiction, however, have been far more surprising and amusing, to *me*, at least. I may actually have done some sort of growing up in that field. That would be nice, if that were so. It might prove that works of the imagination themselves have the power to create.

If a person with a demonstrably ordinary mind, like mine, will devote himself to giving birth to a work of the imagination, that work will in turn tempt and tease that ordinary mind into cleverness. A painter friend, James

Preface

Brooks, told me last summer, "I put the first brush stroke on the canvas. After that, it is up to the canvas to do at least half the work." The same might be said for writing paper and clay and film and vibrating air, and for all the other lifeless substances human beings have managed to turn into teachers and playmates.

I am speaking mostly about Americans. I don't know much about other countries. And I thought for a while that Americans might actually increase their wisdom through experiments with their body chemistry, or with meditation techniques borrowed from Asia. I now have to say that all such voyagers have returned to American banality without any artifacts, and with adventure stories stimulating only to themselves.

So I now believe that the only way in which Americans can rise above their ordinariness, can mature sufficiently to rescue themselves and to help rescue their planet, is through enthusiastic intimacy with works of their own imaginations. I am not especially satisfied with my own imaginative works, my fiction. I am simply impressed by the unexpected insights which shower down on me when my job is to imagine, as contrasted with the woodenly familiar ideas which clutter my desk when my job is to tell the truth.

Yours truly,

Wampeters
Foma

Granfalloons

Science
Fiction

Y EARS ago I was working in Schenectady for General Electric, completely surrounded by machines and ideas for machines, so I wrote a novel about people and machines, and machines frequently got the best of it, as machines will. (It was called *Player Piano,* and it was brought out again in both hard cover and paperback.) And I learned from the reviewers that I was a science-fiction writer.

I didn't know that. I supposed that I was writing a novel about life, about things I could not avoid seeing and hearing in Schenectady, a very real town, awkwardly set in the gruesome now. I have been a soreheaded occupant of a file drawer labeled "science fiction" ever since, and I would like out, particularly since so many serious critics regularly mistake the drawer for a urinal.

The way a person gets into this drawer, apparently, is to notice technology. The feeling persists that no one can simultaneously be a respectable writer and understand how a refrigerator works, just as no gentleman wears a brown suit in the city. Colleges may be to blame. English majors are encouraged, I know, to hate chemistry and physics, and to be proud because they are not dull and creepy and humorless and war-oriented like the engineers across the quad. And our most impressive critics have commonly been such English majors, and they are squeamish about technology to this very day. So it is natural for them to despise science fiction.

But there are those who adore being classified as science-fiction writers anyway, who are alarmed by the possibility that they might someday be known simply as ordinary short-story writers and novelists who mention, among other things, the fruits of engineering and research. They are happy with the *status quo* because their colleagues love them the way members of old-fashioned big families were supposed to do. Science-fiction writers meet often, comfort and praise one another, exchange single-spaced letters of twenty pages and more, booze it up affectionately, and one way or another have a million heart-throbs and laughs.

I have run with them some, and they are generous and amusing souls, but I must now make a true statement that will put them through the roof: They are joiners. They are a lodge. If they didn't enjoy having a gang of their own so much, there would be no such category as science fiction. They love to stay up all night, arguing the question, "What is science fiction?" One might as usefully inquire, "What are the Elks? And what is the Order of the Eastern Star?"

Well—it would be a drab world without meaningless social aggregations. There would be a lot fewer smiles, and about one-hundredth as many publications. And there is this to be said for the science-fiction publications: If somebody can write just a little bit, they will probably publish him. In the Golden Age of Magazines, which wasn't so long ago, inexcusable trash was in such great demand that it led to the invention of the electric typewriter, and incidentally financed my escape from Schenectady. Happy days! But there is now only one sort of magazine to which a maundering sophomore may apply for instant recognition as a writer. Guess what sort.

Which is not to say that the editors of science-fiction magazines and anthologies and novels are tasteless. They are not tasteless, and I will get to them by and by. The people in the field who can be charged fairly with tastelessness are 75 percent of the writers and 95 percent of the readers—or not so much tastelessness, really, as childishness. Mature relationships, even with machines, do not titillate the unwashed majority. Whatever it knows about science was fully revealed in *Popular Mechanics* by 1933. Whatever it knows about politics and economics and history can be found in the *Information Please Almanac* for 1941. Whatever it knows about the relationship between men and women derives mainly from the clean and the pornographic versions of "Maggie and Jiggs."

I taught for a while in a mildly unusual school for mildly unusual high-school children, and current science fiction was catnip to the boys, any science fiction at all. They couldn't tell one story from another, thought they were all neat, keen. What appealed to them so, I think, aside from the novelty of comic books without pictures, was the steady promise of futures which they, *just as they were,* could handle. In such futures they would be high-ranking noncoms at the very least, *just as they were,* pimples, virginity, and everything.

Curiously, the American space program did not excite them. This was not because the program was too mature for them. On the contrary, they were charmingly aware that it was manned and financed by tone-deaf adolescents like themselves. They were simply being realistic: They doubted that they would ever graduate from high school, and they knew that any creep hoping to enter the program would have to have a B.S. degree at a minimum, and that the really good jobs went to creeps with Ph.D.s.

Most of them *did* graduate from high school, by the way. And many of them now cheerfully read about futures and presents and even pasts which nobody can handle— *1984, Invisible Man, Madame Bovary.* They are particularly hot for Kafka. Boomers of science fiction might reply, "Ha! Orwell and Ellison and Flaubert and Kafka are science-fiction writers, too!" They often say things like that. Some are crazy enough to try to capture Tolstoy. It is as though I were to claim that everybody of note belonged fundamentally to Delta Upsilon, my own lodge, incidentally, whether he knew it or not. Kafka would have been a desperately unhappy D.U.

But listen—about the editors and anthologists and publishers who keep the science-fiction field separate and alive: They are uniformly brilliant and sensitive and well-informed. They are among the precious few Americans in whose minds C. P. Snow's two cultures sweetly intertwine. They publish so much bad stuff because good stuff is hard to find, and because they feel it is their duty to encourage any writer, no matter how frightful, who has guts enough to include technology in the human equation. Good for them. They want buxom images of the new reality.

And they get them from time to time, too. Along with the worst writing in America, outside of the education journals, they publish some of the best. They are able to get a few really excellent stories, despite low budgets and an immature readership, because to a few good writers the artificial category, the file drawer labeled "science fiction," will always be home. These writers are rapidly becoming old men, and deserve to be called grand. They are not without honors. The lodge gives them honors all the time. And love.

The lodge will dissolve. All lodges do, sooner or later. And more and more writers in "the mainstream," as science-fiction people call the world outside the file drawer, will include technology in their tales, will give it at least the respect due in a narrative to a wicked stepmother. Meanwhile, if you write stories that are weak on dialogue and motivation and characterization and common sense, you could do worse than throw in a little chemistry or physics, or even witchcraft, and mail them off to the science-fiction magazines.

Brief Encounters on the Inland Waterway

THE fifty-one-foot motor yacht *Marlin* is a period piece, built for Edsel Ford in 1930. Her boxy mahogany-and-glass superstructure, her forward cockpit, with a Stutz Bearcat windshield all its own, and her rumrunner hull cry out for Jimmy Walker and Texas Guinan to come aboard. But for the past nine years she has been the beamy, airy, highly practical day boat of Joseph P. Kennedy and his many descendants. And though political conferences of pith and moment have taken place on her from time to time, her passengers during her Hyannis Port summers are mostly children.

The ship, hull No. 132, has had about eight owners since 1930. She was designed by Eldredge-McInnis, Inc., and built by F. D. Lawley, Inc., both of Quincy, Massachusetts. She is driven by two big Chrysler Imperial engines—225 horsepower. Her lockers are crammed with water skis, fishing tackle, and unclaimed sneakers of every size. Under a seat cushion is a family flag—a white pennant with two large, rose-colored stars at its center and nine smaller stars across the top.

The *Marlin*'s captain, Frank Wirtanen of West Barnstable, Cape Cod, says of his present duties, "I don't think a man without children of his own, without a real understanding of children, could hold this job very long without going bananas."

Captain Wirtanen is a graduate of the Massachusetts Maritime Academy. He used to command tankers, both in peace and in war. He now has the Kennedy yacht fitted out with a system of rubber mats and scuppers that make it possible for him to hose away the remains of chocolate cake and peanut-butter-and-jelly sandwiches in a fairly short time.

Not long ago, Captain Wirtanen asked me to be his crew of one when he took his famous ship on her annual autumn run from Hyannis Port to West Palm Beach, down the Inland Waterway. It is a trip many millionaires' vessels make every year, almost never with a millionaire on board.

"Yes I will," I told him. "Yes."

Call me Molly Bloom. Call me Ishmael.

I am a fool when it comes to money. I agreed to work for a very modest fee plus all I could cook and eat, which turned out to be plenty. I think I ate so much because of my anxiety over which was port and which was starboard. Frank insisted on speaking of everything in nautical terms.

Frank slept in the after cabin, which looked like the master stateroom from outside, with venetian blinds on the windows. Actually, it was the engine room, and Frank slept on a hammock slung over the two sky-blue Chryslers.

I slept on a narrow bunk in the main cabin. There was a two-burner gas range, an old-fashioned icebox, a china cabinet with leaded glass doors that had bellied out, and a sink with a bowl the size of a derby.

"All due respect to the Kennedys," I said, "but this would make a wonderful set for a Clifford Odets play about the Great Depression. 'The curtain rises on the kitchen of a railroad flat on the Lower East Side.'"

The bridge was a drafty, canvas-curtained affair. More modern vessels have the controls in a living room, integrated into the stereo-TV console, with the binnacle concealed in a clump of plastic pachysandra.

We had only a radio to entertain us. It had a standard broadcast band, but Frank wasn't interested. His idea of show business was the distress band. All it did the livelong day was fizz and crackle. Occasionally somebody would call the Coast Guard to ask if he could be heard. That was it.

"Don't you want to hear the political news?" I asked.

As skipper of the *Marlin,* Frank had met a lot of major political figures—Johnson, all the Kennedys, of course, and I don't know who all. "Aren't you curious about how all your famous friends are making out?"

"What?"

"Never mind."

The Inland Waterway, in one form or another, runs all over the country, of course. The stretch we were using was a system of bays, lakes, rivers, and creeks very close to the open Atlantic, dredged to a depth of twelve feet, linked by canals, and marked as plainly as the aisles of a well-run supermarket. "Slow—Congested Area," say signs along the way, or "All Credit Cards Honored at Bill and Thelma's Sunoco Marina, 8 Miles," and so on.

What with drawbridges and tight bends and speed limits and traffic, it is a slow way to travel—our trip took fourteen days—but an amusing, often lovely, and very safe way, too.

It is not a single artery. There are many forks and byways, plenty of choices to be made. It is not under the jurisdiction of a single government body, but is variously maintained by a patchwork of federal and state agencies and often, away from the main channels, by private enterprises.

Some romantics say the Waterway extends all the way to Maine. This I deny, for Frank and I nearly lost the *Marlin* with all hands in October chops on Buzzards Bay and Long Island Sound. We went through New York City on a tide of boiling orange peels, had to take Sandy Hook on the outside, since there is no inside route, and did not see still waters until we had cut through a rolling rip to gain the harbor at Manasquan, New Jersey.

In point of serenity, there the Waterway truly begins.

The *Marlin* was recognized in Manasquan. She had been in plenty of news pictures and she had a Kennedy rakishness to her. She was easy to spot.

I was gassing her up and an old man came limping down the dock, chewing on an unlighted pipe. He watched for some time before he spoke.

"Kennedy boat?" he said at last.

"Yes."

"Taking her to Washington, D.C.?"

"West Palm."

He nodded with rueful wisdom. "All comes to the same thing," he said.

Frank and I went bombing along the outside the next day, because the weather was nice. The Waterway keeps offering glimpses of the outside. The thing to do, unless you're on a honeymoon, is to take the outside whenever things look reasonable. That way you can really make time.

So as it turned out, I didn't get to see much of the Jersey inland stretch. Frank said I would have laughed like hell, chugging through people's backyards.

We cut through the Cape May Canal, headed up Delaware Bay. We were stopped by an Army Corps of Engineers patrol boat at the mouth of the Chesapeake and Delaware Canal. The lieutenant in command wanted to know how long we were, how much water we drew, and so on. We told him we drew a shade more than three feet, and so on.

"Owner?" the lieutenant asked.

The answer was fairly complicated, since the *Marlin* is technically owned by a business associate of Mr. Kennedy. Frank gave the name.

"His address?"

"Care of Joseph P. Kennedy, Hyannis Port, Massachusetts," said Frank.

The shavetail didn't show a flicker of recognition. "Street address there?"

"They don't have street addresses there," said Frank. "It's just a little country town. Everybody knows everybody."

W e spent the night at a marina on the canal, gassed up again, took aboard 160 gallons. Frank made a calculation. "We're getting better than a mile to the gallon."

"That's *good,* Frank?"

"It's *splendid.*"

When we got to West Palm, I added up all the gasoline we'd bought: It came to 1,522 gallons.

T here are marinas sprinkled conveniently all the way down the Waterway. No one is ever very far from fuel or a mechanic—though the mechanics are often poor.

"The average household has more tools than *he* does," I heard Frank say about one mechanic. "He couldn't put the cap back on his Four Roses without crossing the threads."

Brief Encounters on the Inland Waterway

Marinas that do a big business with transients are essentially filling stations. They make their money from the sale of fuel. The average charge for overnight dockage is about seven cents a foot—ridiculously low, considering that free electricity and water and showers and television rooms and so on are generally thrown in.

Like ordinary filling stations, marinas can be anything from sparkling clean to unbelievably foul. The newest charts show where they are and tell what conveniences are offered. A general rule: The farther south you go, the more luxurious the marinas become. Naturally.

And it isn't necessary to spend every night in a marina: There is such a thing as an anchor.

It was in the Chesapeake and Delaware Canal that Frank and I met with a gaggle of millionaires' yachts heading south. There must have been at least twenty of them in the marina, and some of them could have used the *Marlin* for a lifeboat.

There was a medallion on our dashboard that said, "Oh God, Thy sea is so great, and my boat is so small!" When I first read that I said to myself, "Still and all, fifty-one feet is a pretty fair size." It is nothing.

There weren't any millionaires around, but the millionaires' captains, cooks, and crewmen were regaling themselves at Schaefer's, a famous seafood restaurant. A roomful of professional sailors is a disconcerting thing to see. Nobody looks at anybody else. Everybody is scanning the horizon.

We sat down with an old friend of Frank's, a Nova

Scotian named Bert. He was sixty years old, had bright blue eyes and the complexion of a used footlocker. He was master of the *Charity Anne Browning,* a sixty-eight-foot yawl. He and Frank had known each other for fifteen years. Frank knew his first name but not his last, which put Frank one up on Bert. Bert didn't know anybody's name, first or last. He called everybody "Captain." Even me. When I denied that I was one, he stopped including me in the conversation. I didn't know then that everybody on the Waterway is "Captain." Deny that you are a captain and you will disappear.

Bert had us aboard the *Charity Anne Browning* for a drink, along with a deeply unhappy Swede named Gunther. Gunther was captain of the *Golden Hind VI,* a baby ocean liner that towered over the *Marlin* like the City of God.

The *Charity Anne Browning* looked from the outside like a very businesslike sailing vessel, possibly engaged in the copra trade. Below decks she was like the bridal suite in the newest motor lodge in Reno—thick carpets, three tiled baths, a fifteen-foot couch covered with panther skin, and steam heat. In the owner's cabin there was a king-size bed with the covers turned back. The sheets and pillow-cases were dotted with forget-me-nots.

The sails were never raised. The ship had a big, hairy diesel that could make her plane. As Frank said later, "She needs sails about as much as an atomic submarine."

Bert kept the ship immaculate inside by the simple expedient of not letting anybody use anything. He kept us off the couch. I made the mistake of using an ashtray, and he took it away immediately, washed it, and put it carefully into a cupboard.

Late that night, I saw Bert and his crew of two going down the icy dock to use the marina's toilets rather than dirty their own.

When I saw the bed turned down, I asked Bert if he was expecting the owner aboard. He said he didn't think he would see the owner for at least another three months.

"Owner?" said Gunther. He was feeling pretty good. "What the hell is an owner? What does one of *those* look like?"

"You never see your owner?" I asked.

"Oh, sure, all the time—two hours last year, fifteen minutes the year before that. Last time I wrote him, I said, 'Hey, how about a recent photograph?' This is a real crazy country. Thousands of yachts are being built every year for people who just don't want to get *on* them. Why do they want them? Maybe so they can tell a dame, 'I got a boat with a captain and everything.' "

"Your owner answers letters?"

"Oh, sure. 'Take the ship up to Bar Harbor,' he says. 'Take her down to Miami. Take her through the Strait of Magellan and paint her sky blue.' "

Gunther rolled his eyes. "The pay is good. I even get raises. But every so often I wake up in the middle of the night and I whisper to myself, 'Hey, Gunther, what the hell you think you're doing?' "

The luxury fleet did not stick together during the daytime. We strung out down Chesapeake Bay. There were no agreements as to where next we would meet. There was a certain amount of lazy navigation, one skipper following another rather than bothering with charts, compass readings, and all that.

Frank warned me against following anybody. "Thinking the guy up ahead knows what he's doing is the most dangerous religion there is," he said. He told me that a lot of the yachts were being taken to Florida by wild kids, often relatives of the owners, who were out for kicks.

A little later in the day we cut our speed to ten knots because of a crack in an exhaust manifold (we normally cruised at fifteen). We were passed by a three-bedroom Chris-Craft doing about thirty. Her skipper was calling us on the distress band, which we had tuned in, of course. But I had gone deaf to the thing and Frank was below.

"Hey, *Marlin,* wake up! *Marlin.* Come on, now, *Marlin* —answer, boy!"

Frank finally heard it, responded. "This is the yacht *Marlin.*"

"Listen, yacht *Marlin*—you got some charts?"

"Yes."

"You mind giving me some general idea where I am?"

He got his information, but four days later we saw the ship again, up on a marine railway in Elizabeth City, North Carolina. Both of her propellers and her rudder were gone.

North of Norfolk the Inland Waterway has a raw and practical feel. The traffic is dense and businesslike. The shores teem and smoke and clang with industries. South of Norfolk, particularly along the slow route, the antique route, which is the Dismal Swamp Canal, the way narrows, the trees overhang, the climate softens, becomes sweetly malarial. For the first time, it is possible to have the fantasy of being Huck Finn.

Frank and I took off our jackets, rolled up our sleeves and the canvas curtains on the bridge. We bought jars of swamp honey from a lock tender. While the lock was filling up, word got around that the Kennedy yacht was passing through.

"You ain't got that Bobby on there, have you?" somebody called jeeringly from the shore.

"No," said Frank. He explained to me, "We're in the South now."

The voluptuous miasma of uninhabitable Southern swamps was virtually continuous, all the way to the Florida line. There were melodramatic mud flats and snags to avoid. The water looked like coffee, and what birds we saw! I told Frank I was pleased to learn that so much of the Eastern Seaboard was still wilderness. I also found a lot of the trip boring as hell.

Frank and I eased the monotony some by eating like pigs and blowing the horn at cormorants on the channel markers. "Get the hell off my marker!" Frank would yell, and he would blow the horn, and we would both be eating liverwurst or swamp-honey sandwiches or some damn stuff that was supposed to help Frank get over an operation for an ulcer.

One day we passed a ketch with her sails up. The man at the tiller had blubber hanging all over him. He was grotesquely fat, but ruddy, and his expression was manly, as though he had plenty of hard, dangerous work to do. "Yachting," said Frank, with his mouth full, "isn't really the athletic event some people make it out to be."

The best part of the trip was walking around unfamiliar cities and towns and villages in the evening—Elizabeth City, Morehead City, Myrtle Beach, Charleston, Isle of Hope, Jacksonville, Cocoa, and finally West Palm.

I will never forget a fragment of conversation I overheard in Charleston, South Carolina: "There is a woman who won't even look at me on the street. But I can call her up on the telephone and she will talk to me for hours."

There had been a lot of sly talk before we set out on our voyage about how women would be falling all over Frank and me when we pulled into marina after marina in a Kennedy yacht. But women are a rare sight around yacht basins. "Women only pretend to like boats—to hook a man who owns one," a skipper told me. "A boat to your average woman is just one more damn house to take care of, only it's more uncomfortable, and the man orders her around like Captain Bligh, and she doesn't trust the machinery or the plumbing, and she has to walk six blocks to buy groceries or get the laundry done."

Frank and I entered into a fairly deep conversation with only one woman in a marina. She didn't fall all over us with admiration. She was a Goldwater fan, for one thing. For another, she was singlehandedly running a boat bigger than ours, taking it all the way from Ithaca, New York, to Key West.

We congratulated her on her courage and seamanship and yellow foul-weather gear.

"Back home," she said, "they call me Barnacle Bill."

I asked her why she admired Goldwater.

"Any man who can fly his own plane, do his own navigation, repair his own radio, and develop his own film is A Number One in *my* book."

18

Whenever a marina operator recognized the *Marlin,* he would call up the local paper. He and Frank and the boat and I would then get our picture in the paper. But the nicest recognition came from a Negro who took our lines in Jacksonville.

"Oh, my goodness," he said, "is this the President's boat? Was this Mr. Kennedy's?"

To keep things simple, we said it was. He patted the boat affectionately, shook his head. "I got to tell my wife about this. This is the best thing ever happened to me."

When we got to West Palm, Gunther, the unhappy Swede, was there to greet us. His little ocean liner had beat the *Marlin* by three hours.

"Here we are," said Frank.

"And who cares?" answered Gunther gloomily. "Look! All the shutters are still up. Nobody will be down here for another two months. When they do come down, nobody's going to be crazy enough to get on a boat."

Frank pointed out that the Kennedys used the *Marlin* a great deal.

"They're out of their minds," said Gunther. "How did you like our great Inland Waterway?" he asked me.

"Well—" I said, "I'd like to take it a lot slower next time. I'd like to explore and fish, anchor in creeks, wake up with the birds all around. A very beautiful life is certainly possible on the Inland Waterway for anybody who has the time."

"First," said Gunther, "get yourself a yacht."

Hello,
Star
Vega*

COMEDY of the most pleasant sort is represented by this collaboration between Carl Sagan of Harvard and Iosef Shmuelovich Shklovskii of the Sternberg Astronomical Institute in Russia. It wasn't supposed to be a collaboration at first, but it just worked out that way: So enthusiastically did Dr. Sagan annotate the American edition of Shklovskii's *Vselennaia, Zhiza, Razum (Universe, Life, Mind)* that he became coauthor. That was all right with Shklovskii, who fattened the book even more by annotating Sagan's annotations. The result is a stunningly authoritative book about the universe, meant to be read by common men.

Sample sentence: "Why does the sun shine?" Another:

Review of Intelligent Life in the Universe *by I. S. Shklovskii and Carl Sagan*

"Imagine the universe as an unbaked raisin cake." To which Sagan adds, "Worse analogies have been made."

The coauthors have never met. The Russian has written to the American that "the probability of our meeting is unlikely to be smaller than the probability of a visit to the Earth by an extraterrestrial cosmonaut." Their not meeting has nothing to do with politics. It's just that neither astronomer is a traveling man. Incidentally, the probability of our someday having a visitor from outer space, or perhaps of our having had one already, is a good deal more thrilling than zero. The authors calculate that there may be enough advanced technical civilizations in the universe to pay Earth a call every thousand years or so.

Let me hasten to say: They are quite certain that we are not being visited now. Sagan served this year on a committee that reviewed the handling by the Air Force of UFO reports, and he is able to state:

> The saucer myths represent a neat compromise between the need to believe in a traditional paternal God and the contemporary pressures to accept the pronouncements of science. . . . Repeated sightings of UFOs and the persistence of the United States Air Force and members of the responsible scientific community in explaining the sightings away have suggested to some that a conspiracy exists to conceal from the public the true nature of the UFOs. But precisely because people desire so intensely that unidentified flying objects be of a benign, intelligent, and extraterrestrial origin, honesty requires that . . . we accept only the most rigorous logic and the most convincing evidence.

In that spirit, Shklovskii and Sagan deny that there is any good evidence, outside of a mathematical probability, that we have ever been visited.

It is in the future that the real sensations lie. The authors, cautious about so many things, virtually promise that Earthlings will one day be exploring the whole Milky Way at velocities approaching that of light. They talk about interstellar ramjets that will feed on atoms scattered through space, about antimatter as fuel, contained in magnetic bottles, of course. They patiently explain to me again what I am too dumb to understand ever: why hearts and clocks naturally slow down as they approach the speed of light, why time on spaceships isn't anything like time on my mantelpiece.

I believe all this, and much, much more, because I guess it is my duty to. But I pay a price for my gaga credulity, which I want to describe as a sort of intellectual seasickness.

Of the two collaborators, it is the American astronomer who is the more humane writer, who, with friendly, wry little asides, acknowledges that the reader might, for good reasons, be nauseated and scared stiff. Dr. Sagan has seen fit to include as illustrations, along with flabbergasting photographs of galaxies and double stars, cartoons by Charles Schulz and Charles Addams which relate human beings (and Snoopy) to the universe humbly. Dr. Shklovskii, on the other hand, is a sort of heedless Tom Swift with trillions of rubles to spend.

Man's intelligence, by the way, has already effected a radical change in the solar system. Earth has suddenly become a powerful source of radio energy. "Thus," says

Sagan the humanist, "the characteristic signs of life on Earth which may be detectable over interstellar distances include the baleful contents of many American television programs." It is a sobering thought that Gomer Pyle and the Beverly Hillbillies may be among our chief interstellar emissaries.

Teaching
the
Unteachable

YOU can't teach people to write well. Writing well is something God lets you do or declines to let you do. Most bright people know that, but writers' conferences continue to multiply in the good old American summertime. Sixty-eight of them are listed in last April's issue of *The Writer*. Next year there will be more. They are harmless. They are shmoos.

I saw one born five years ago—The Cape Cod Writers' Conference in Craigville, Massachusetts. It was more or less prayed into existence by three preachers' wives. They were in middle life. They invited some Cape writers and English teachers to a meeting one winter night, and their spokeswoman said this: "We thought it would be nice if there were a writers' conference on Cape Cod next summer."

I remember another thing she said: "We thought established writers would probably enjoy helping beginners like us to break into the field."

And it came to pass. Isaac Asimov is the star this year. Stars of the past include Richard Kim and Jacques Barzun. Twenty-six students came the first year, forty-three the next, sixty-three the next, eighty-two the next, and nearly one hundred are expected this year—in August. Most of the students are women. Several of them are preachers' wives in middle life.

So it goes.

I congratulated one of the founders recently, and she replied, "Well, it's been an awful lot of fun for all of us. Writers lead such lonely lives, you know, so they really enjoy getting together once a year to discuss matters of common interest."

That's the most delightful part of the game, of course: the pretense that everybody who comes to a writers' conference is a writer. Other forms of innocent summer recreation immediately suggest themselves: a doctors' conference, where everybody gets to pretend to be a doctor; a lawyers' conference, where everybody gets to pretend to be a lawyer; and so on—and maybe even a Kennedy conference, where everybody pretends to be somehow associated with the Kennedys.

"Who comes to writers' conferences?" you ask. A random sample of twenty students will contain six recent divorcées, three wives in middle life, five schoolteachers of no particular age or sex, two foxy grandmas, one sweet old widower with true tales to tell about railroading in Idaho, one real writer, one not merely angry but absolutely furious young man, and one physician with forty years' worth of privileged information that he wants to sell to the movies for a blue million.

"How much sex is there at writers' conferences?" you ask. The staff members, at any rate, don't come for sex. They hate conferences. They come for money. They are zombies. They want to collect their paychecks and go home. There are exceptions, who only prove the rule.

I saw another writers' conference born only this past June 18. I pick that date, since that was when the Student-Faculty Get-Acquainted Party was held. It was The West-Central Writers' Conference, sponsored by Western Illinois University, which is in Macomb, Illinois. The party was held in the TraveLodge Motel in Macomb, in between the Coin-A-Wash and the A & W Rootbeer stand, because there was booze. There is a rule against booze on campus.

The founder and director wasn't a preacher's wife. He was a cigar-eating young English instructor named E. W. Johnson. In the conference brochure he claimed to have been a secondhand-clothing salesman, a construction worker, and a professional gambler. He is also a novelist and a writer of textbooks, and the only teacher at Western Illinois who has published a book. Johnson was sad at the party because he had sent out thousands of brochures and had advertised lavishly in *Writer's Digest* and *Saturday Review* and so on, and yet only nineteen students had come. They were sitting around the room, rolling their eyes moonily, waiting for new friendships to begin.

"I can't understand it," he said above the Muzak and the sounds of drag races out on Route 136. "We have as good a staff as any conference in the country."

And the staff really was at least fair to middling. There was myself, described in the brochure as "the foremost black humorist in American fiction"; and there was Richard Yates, "perhaps the greatest living short-story writer in America"; and there was John Clellon Holmes, "the official biographer of the Beat Generation, who has recently completed a novel entitled 'Perfect Fools,' which is written from a 'white humor' point of view"; and there was Frederic Will, "one of the most versatile writers in America, having published extensively (eighteen books) in the fields of poetry, nonfiction and translation."

Johnson confessed that it had appeared for a while that only five students were coming, and he blurted, too, that he had never been to a writers' conference before.

I asked him how he had come to found such a thing, and he said that he sure wasn't doing it for money. All he was getting as director was his regular instructor's pay. He honestly wanted to help writers.

The party died at midnight. Everybody had gone home by then except Johnson and a couple of staff members and a girl who had been recently divorced—from an Arab, she said. We were sitting around the swimming pool, breathing chlorine and carbon monoxide.

"You know why more people didn't come?" said the girl.

"Nope," said Johnson.

"Because 'Macomb, Illinois' sounds like such a hellhole, and because 'Western Illinois University' sounds like such a jerkwater school," she explained.

Her point was a sound one. The most agreeable writers' conference would be conducted in Acapulco under the joint auspices of Harvard and Oxford, with everybody's getting a writer's license after a week or so.

Teaching the Unteachable

The most respectable summer conference I know of, though, takes place in a hell-hole a lot like Macomb, which is Bloomington, Indiana. There *is* an excellent university there, of course, Indiana University, the conference host. And what I find so admirable in Bloomington is the insistence that no would-be writer can learn much or improve much in one silly week, and that anybody who is serious about entering the trade had better come back year after year for evaluation, and to write his head off in between.

We four superstars at the fiasco in Macomb were all teachers or ex-teachers from the Writers' Workshop at the University of Iowa, where the students are trapped for years rather than days. E. W. Johnson got his Master of Fine Arts degree there. I have quit after two years—not angrily, but feeling waterlogged. I got no work of my own done there. The students, hand-picked from all over the country, were generally so talented and productive and responsive that working with them filled the days and nights to brimming. And the hell with that.

"How did you help them?" you ask.

Well—the Workshop itself made writing fiction seem a dignified and useful enterprise by forming a community of writers, something writers even in New York City can't find in their hometowns. It provided them with successful professional writers as tutors, whose purpose was to encourage them and warn them about bonehead mistakes.

As for myself: I tried to help those good students become what they were born to become, and to avoid intimidating them with masterpieces written by great men much older than they were. In a rather alarming manner of speaking, I tried to reach into their mouths without being bitten or tripping their epiglottises. Again in a manner of speaking, I wanted to take hold of the end of a spool of ticker tape in the back of each student's throat. I meant to pull if out inch by inch, so the student and I could read it. The student's literary destiny, which had nothing to do with me or the University of Iowa, was written on the tape.

There were no opportunities for such fancy laryngology at Macomb—or at any summer camp.

Yes,
We Have
No
Nirvanas

UNITARIAN
minister heard that I had been to see Maharishi Mahesh
Yogi, guru to The Beatles and Donovan and Mia Farrow,
and he asked me, "Is he a fake?" His name is Charley.
Unitarians don't believe in anything. I am a Unitarian.

"No," I said. "It made me happy just to see him. His
vibrations are lovely and profound. He teaches that man
was not born to suffer and will not suffer if he practices
Transcendental Meditation, which is easy as pie."

"I can't tell whether you're kidding or not."

"I better *not* be kidding, Charley."

"Why do you say that so grimly?"

"Because my wife and eighteen-year-old daughter are hooked. They've both been initiated. They meditate several times a day. Nothing pisses them off anymore. They glow like bass drums with lights inside."

I saw Maharishi in Cambridge, Massachusetts, after my daughter got hooked, before my wife got hooked, and on the very day that Mia Farrow got hooked. This was last January. Miss Farrow had been suggesting for about a year that she was a Transcendental Meditator, but that was the bunk. She had merely been *hankering* to be one. You can't be the real thing without an initiation.

And not just any Transcendental Meditator can turn you on. Maharishi has to do it, which would be a great honor, or one of the few teachers he has trained. Miss Farrow got the great honor in Maharishi's hotel room in Cambridge. My wife and daughter had to make do with a teacher in the apartment of a Boston painter and jazz musician who meditates.

There is private stuff, but no secret stuff in the initiation. You go to several public lectures first, which are cheerful and encouraging. You are told lovingly that this thing is easy, never fails to make a person more blissful and virtuous and effective, if it is done correctly. The lecturer does not explain what meditation feels like because he cannot. It must be *experienced,* he says.

So you ask for an interview with the teacher, and during that he asks you a little about yourself. He will want to know if you are on drugs or drunk or under psychiatric treatment or plain crazy. You have to be clean and sober and sane, or you won't be initiated. If you're under treatment for mental kinks, you will be told to come back when the treatment is complete.

If the teacher thinks you're okay, you're told to go to a certain address at such and such a time, and to bring as gifts a handkerchief, some fresh fruit, some flowers, and seventy-five dollars. If you are a student or a housewife, you bring thirty-five dollars.

So I have seventy dollars invested in this new religion so far. Maharishi says that his thing is not a religion but a *technique*. Still, at cocktail parties every so often, I can be heard to say sulkily, often within earshot of my wife or daughter, "I've got seventy goddamn simoleons in this new religion so far."

The money goes into traveling expenses for the Master and his teachers, and they don't live very high, and a decent set of books is kept, and the books are open. This is not Southern California-style religion. Sergeant Friday is not about to appear.

Only you and your teacher are present at your initiation into this thing that, to its followers, is so definitely *not* a religion. And there is candlelight and incense, and there are small pictures of Maharishi and his deceased Master, who was His Divinity Swami Brahmananda Saraswati, Jagadguru Bhagwan Shankaracharya of Jyotir Math.

Your teacher, most likely a fellow American in a business suit, will give you your own private *mantra,* a sound which, when contemplated, will begin your descent into your own mind. This giving of sounds, usually Sanskrit words, is the teacher's especial art, or, I beg your pardon, *science.*

My wife asked a teacher how he knew what sound to give to each person, and he said it was a complex thing to explain. "But, believe me," he said, "it is a science."

That science sure worked for her. The instant she heard her *mantra* for the first time, down, down, down she went, free diving in her mind. There is rapture in those depths. Everybody who has been down there says so. And many of Maharishi's mind divers speak as experts when they say the rapture is infinitely more beautiful and revealing than any jag.

And the fuzz can't bust you.

This new religion (which-is-not-a-religion-but-a-technique) offers tremendous pleasure, opposes no existing institutions or attitudes, demands no sacrifices or outward demonstrations of virtue, and is risk free. It will sweep the middle classes of the world as the planet dies—as the planet is surely dying—of poisoned air and water.

The publicity has been spectacular. Last January, when I asked to interview His Holiness, which is the proper term of address for Maharishi, I was told by an aide to come to his hotel in Cambridge "at once." He didn't care who I was, not that I *am* anybody. I was simply more publicity. Transcendental Meditators want all the publicity they can get, because they honestly believe that the technique can save the world.

How?

Unless one is happy, one cannot be at peace [says Maharishi in *The Science of Being and Art of Living* (International Spiritual Regeneration Movement Publications, 1966)]. All the praiseworthy aims of the United Nations only scratch the surface of the problem of world peace. If the minds and resources of statesmen in all countries could be used to popularize and effectively bring to individuals the practice of Transcendental Meditation, the face of the world would be changed overnight. . . . As long as statesmen remain ignorant of the possibility of improving the lives of individuals from within and thereby bringing them abundant peace, happiness, and creative intelligence, the problem of world peace will always be dealt with only on the surface, and the world will continue to suffer its cold and hot wars.

"What do you do about somebody like Lyndon Johnson or George Wallace?" I asked a follower at Maharishi's hotel. We were in a mostly young, all-white crowd milling outside the Master's locked door. The boy I asked was a Boston University student and guitar player. "You expect to get *them* to *meditate?*"

"Even if they don't," he said, "they will still change for the better because people all around them will be changing for the better through Transcendental Meditation."

So there is another attractive feature of the new religion: Every time you dive into your own mind, you are actually dealing effectively with the issues of the day.

There was a middle-aged lady outside the door who wanted to talk to the Master in order to find out if she was meditating correctly. She didn't think so. Diving into her mind, I gathered, was about as much fun as dogpaddling across Cleveland's Cuyahoga River.

"Is it *dangerous* not to do it right?" I asked her. "Could people get sick or go crazy?"

"No, no," she said. "The worst that can happen is that you might be disappointed." That's a long way from being hung up on a cross or thrown to the lions.

35

And an aide came up to me with an armload of newspapers and magazines, which he said I could have. There were big articles about Maharishi in all of them—*Look, Life, Time, Newsweek, The National Observer,* the Boston *Herald Traveler,* the Boston *Globe, The New York Times Magazine.* There were three big news stories that week: heart transplants, the capture of the *Pueblo,* and Maharishi. Maharishi had also made enchanting appearances on *The Today Show,* Johnny Carson's *Tonight Show,* and National Educational Television.

I said to the aide, "With all this publicity, thousands of people are going to want to do this thing right away. Is there some book or pamphlet they can get?"

"No," he said, "and there never will be. A teacher has to *show* you how to experience the subtle states of thinking, and then he has to check your experiences as you proceed down the path."

"Look," I said, "can't I go to a meditator and say, 'Come on, tell me how you do it, and then I'll do it the same way'?"

"You'll be disappointed," he said.

The boy from Boston University chimed in. He said he knew a girl who gave her boyfriend her *mantra.* You're not supposed to tell anybody what your *mantra* is, but this girl did it.

"Is that a *terrible* thing to do?" I asked.

The boy and the aide shrugged. "There are no *terrible* things you can do. It was an *unwise* thing to do," said the aide.

I was still curious. "What happened to the boyfriend when he used his girl's *mantra?*"

"He was disappointed."

Yes, We Have No Nirvanas

Maharishi came out of his room, having meditated, and so many reporters had been promised personal interviews that he had to hold a monster press conference in the hotel ballroom. So we went down there, and Maharishi's deerskin was put on a stage, and he sat on that. He played with a bouquet of yellow chrysanthemums, and invited people to ask him anything they liked.

He is a darling man—small, golden-brown, a giggler with a gray beard and broad shoulders and a thick chest. You might guess from his muscular arms and thick wrists that he had done hard labor during most of his fifty-six years. That would be wrong. Maharishi started out to be a physicist, took a Bachelor of Science degree at Allahabad University, Cyril Dunn says in the London *Observer*. Maharishi gives out no information about himself. A monk isn't supposed to.

Right after he graduated, he became a monk, learned from his masters the easy way to meditate. The easy technique, incidentally, wasn't much respected by other gurus, who were trying to achieve bliss by methods notoriously arduous and often grotesque. Maharishi's Master, on his deathbed, told Maharishi to go out into the world and teach the easy thing. This Maharishi has been doing for ten years. At the end of this year, he will go back into seclusion in India as a simple monk, never again to be a public man. He is said to have gathered a quarter of a million followers throughout the world. The teachers among them will continue to turn people on.

So I sat there on a folding chair in the ballroom, with a couple of hundred Transcendental Meditators behind me. I closed my eyes, waited to be wafted to mysterious India by the poetry of this holy man.

37

"Maharishi," said a reporter, "don't you feel a terrible sense of urgency about the state of the world? Don't you think things are getting awfully black awfully fast?"

"You cannot call a room truly black," said His Holiness, "if you know where the light switch is, and you know how to turn it on."

"You say that the mind naturally seeks its own happiness. What's your evidence for this?"

"If a man sits between two radios tuned to different stations," said Maharishi, "he will naturally turn his attention to the program which pleases him most."

"What are your feelings about civil rights?"

"What *are* they?" he asked.

Civil rights were explained to him in terms of black people who, because they were black, couldn't get nice houses or good educations or jobs.

Maharishi replied that any oppressed person could rise by practicing Transcendental Meditation. He would automatically do his job better, and the economy would pay him more, and then he could buy anything he wanted. He wouldn't be oppressed anymore. In other words, he should quit bitching, begin to meditate, grasp his garters, and float into a commanding position in the marketplace, where transactions are always fair.

And I opened my eyes, and I took a hard look at Maharishi. He hadn't wafted me to India. He had sent me back to Schenectady, New York, where I used to be a public-relations man—years and years ago. That was where I had heard other euphoric men talk of the human condition in terms of switches and radios and the fairness of the marketplace. They, too, thought it was ridiculous for people to be unhappy, when there were so many simple things they could do to improve their lot. They, too, had

Bachelor of Science degrees. Maharishi had come all the way from India to speak to the American people like a General Electric engineer.

Maharishi was asked his opinions of Jesus Christ. He had some. He prefaced them with this dependent clause: "From what people have *told* me about Him—"

Here was a man who had unselfishly spent years of his life in American and northern European hotel rooms, teaching Christians how to save the world. There had to be Gideon Bibles in most of those rooms. Yet, Maharishi had never opened one to find out what Jesus said, exactly.

Some searching mind.

He suggested that Jesus might have been onto something like Transcendental Meditation, but that it was garbled and lost by his followers. A few moments later he said that Jesus and the early Christian saints had mistakenly allowed their minds to wander. "You must have control," he said. The wandering minds of Jesus and the saints had led to what Maharishi called "an absurdity," an emphasis on faith.

"Faith, at best," he declared, "can let a man live and die in hope. The churches are driving people away because that is all they have to offer."

We were back in the marketplace again: Churches were offering sugar pills, whereas Maharishi had a nonprescription drug that packed the kick of a siege howitzer. Which will you choose?

I went outside the hotel after that, liking Jesus better than I had ever liked Him before. I wanted to see a crucifix, so I could say to it, "You know why You're up there? It's Your own fault. You should have practiced Transcendental Meditation, which is easy as pie. You would also have been a better carpenter."

And I ran into a Harvard dean I knew. I only know one Harvard dean, and that's the one I ran into. Maharishi had packed Sanders Theater the night before, so Harvard knew all about the Master, and I asked the dean if Transcendental Meditation would be the next student craze.

"A lot of students walked out last night, as you may have noticed," he said.

"That burned up my wife and daughter," I said.

"The students I've heard talking about Maharishi seem to consider his teachings at least slightly beneath them," he went on. "The people who really go for this thing are The Boston Tea Party crowd." The Boston Tea Party is a rhythm-and-blues joint in a red-brick church in Boston's south end. The patrons and musicians are mainly college kids and mainly white. The joint is the home of the so-called "Bosstown Sound," which *Newsweek* says is "anti-hippie and anti-drugs."

"It seems like a very good religion for people who, in troubled times, don't want any trouble," I said.

"There's a Harvard pole-vaulter who claims he is jumping higher and higher all the time, thanks to Maharishi," said the dean.

"And the crowd cheers."

My daughter, who has always been a good artist, says that she is a much better artist now, thanks to Maharishi. My wife, who was a good writer in college, is going to take up writing again. They tell me that I would write much better and be more cheerful about it if I went skin diving into my own mind twice a day.

All that keeps me from becoming a meditator myself is laziness. I would have to get out of the house and go to Boston, and spend several nights there. Also: I doubt that I have the courage and the humorlessness to present myself at somebody's apartment door with fruit, flowers, a clean handkerchief, and a gift of seventy-five dollars.

So I say mean things to my wife like, "What kind of a holy man is it that talks economics like a traveling secretary of the National Association of Manufacturers?"

"People *make* him talk economics. He doesn't want to talk about them. They aren't his field," she says.

"How come he bombed in India, the home of meditators, and then had great success with middle-class people in Scandinavia and West Germany and Great Britain and America?"

"For many complicated reasons, no doubt."

"Maybe it's because he talks economics like a traveling secretary of the National Association of Manufacturers."

"Think what you like," she says, loving me, loving me, loving me. She smiles.

"If this thing is so good," I say, "why doesn't Maharishi take it right into the slums, where people are really suffering?"

"Because he wants to spread the word as fast as possible, and the best way to do that is to start with influential people."

"Like The Beatles."

"Among others."

"I can see where influential people would like Maharishi better than Jesus. My God, if The Beatles and Mia Farrow went to Jesus, He'd tell 'em to give all their money away."

And my wife smiles.

Fortitude

THE TIME: *the present.*
THE PLACE: *Upstate New York, a large room filled with pulsing, writhing, panting machines that perform the functions of various organs of the human body—heart, lungs, liver, and so on. Color-coded pipes and wires swoop upward from the machines to converge and pass through a hole in the ceiling. To one side is a fantastically complicated master control console.*

DR. ELBERT LITTLE, *a kindly, attractive young general practitioner, is being shown around by the creator and boss of the operation,* DR. NORBERT FRANKENSTEIN. FRANKENSTEIN *is 65, a crass medical genius. Seated at the console, wearing headphones and watching meters and flashing lights, is* DR. TOM SWIFT, FRANKENSTEIN *'s enthusiastic first assistant.*

LITTLE: Oh, my God—oh, my God—
FRANKENSTEIN: Yeah. Those are her kidneys over there. That's her liver, of course. There you got her pancreas.

43

LITTLE: Amazing. Dr. Frankenstein, after seeing this, I wonder if I've even been *practicing* medicine, if I've ever even *been* to medical school. *(Pointing)* That's her *heart?*

FRANKENSTEIN: That's a Westinghouse heart. They make a damn good heart, if you ever need one. They make a kidney I wouldn't touch with a ten-foot pole.

LITTLE: That heart is probably worth more than the whole township where I practice.

FRANKENSTEIN: That pancreas is worth your whole state. *Vermont?*

LITTLE: Vermont.

FRANKENSTEIN: What we paid for the pancreas—yeah, we could have bought Vermont for that. Nobody'd ever made a pancreas before, and we had to have one in ten days or lose the patient. So we told all the big organ manufacturers, "OK, you guys got to have a crash program for a pancreas. Put every man you got on the job. We don't care what it costs, as long as we get a pancreas by next Tuesday."

LITTLE: And they succeeded.

FRANKENSTEIN: The patient's still alive, isn't she? Believe me, those are some expensive sweetbreads.

LITTLE: But the patient could afford them.

FRANKENSTEIN: You don't live like this on Blue Cross.

LITTLE: And how many operations has she had? In how many years?

FRANKENSTEIN: I gave her her first major operation thirty-six years ago. She's had seventy-eight operations since then.

LITTLE: And how old is she?

FRANKENSTEIN: One hundred.

LITTLE: What *guts* that woman must have!

FRANKENSTEIN: You're looking at 'em.

LITTLE: I mean—what *courage!* What *fortitude!*

FRANKENSTEIN: We knock her out, you know. We don't operate without anesthetics.

LITTLE: Even so . . .

FRANKENSTEIN *taps* SWIFT *on the shoulder.* SWIFT *frees an ear from the headphones, divides his attention between the visitors and the console.*

FRANKENSTEIN: Dr. Tom Swift, this is Dr. Elbert Little. Tom here is my first assistant.

SWIFT: Howdy-doody.

FRANKENSTEIN: Dr. Little has a practice up in Vermont. He happened to be in the neighborhood. He asked for a tour.

LITTLE: What do you hear in the headphones?

SWIFT: Anything that's going on in the patient's room. *(He offers the headphones)* Be my guest.

LITTLE *(listening to headphones)*: Nothing.

SWIFT: She's having her hair brushed now. The beautician's up there. She's always quiet when her hair's being brushed. *(He takes the headphones back)*

FRANKENSTEIN *(to* SWIFT*)*: We should *congratulate* our young visitor here.

SWIFT: What for?

LITTLE: Good question. What for?

FRANKENSTEIN: Oh, I know about the great honor that has come your way.

LITTLE: I'm not sure *I* do.

FRANKENSTEIN: You are *the* Dr. Little, aren't you, who was named the Family Doctor of the Year by the *Ladies' Home Journal* last month?

LITTLE: Yes—that's right. I don't know how in the hell

they decided. And I'm even more flabbergasted that a man of *your* caliber would know about it.

FRANKENSTEIN: I read the *Ladies' Home Journal* from cover to cover every month.

LITTLE: You *do?*

FRANKENSTEIN: I only got one patient, Mrs. Lovejoy. And Mrs. Lovejoy reads the *Ladies' Home Journal,* so I read it, too. That's what we talk about—what's in the *Ladies' Home Journal.* We read all about you last month. Mrs. Lovejoy kept saying, "Oh, what a nice young man he must be. *So understanding.*"

LITTLE: Um.

FRANKENSTEIN: Now here you are in the flesh. I bet she wrote you a letter.

LITTLE: Yes—she did.

FRANKENSTEIN: She writes thousands of letters a year, gets thousands of letters back. Some pen pal she is.

LITTLE: Is she—uh—generally *cheerful* most of the time?

FRANKENSTEIN: If she isn't, that's our fault down here. If she gets unhappy, that means something down *here* isn't working right. She was blue about a month ago. Turned out it was a bum transistor in the console. (*He reaches over* SWIFT*'s shoulder, changes a setting on the console. The machinery subtly adjusts to the new setting.*) There—she'll be all depressed for a couple of minutes now. (*He changes the setting again) There.* Now, pretty quick, she'll be happier than she was before. She'll sing like a bird.

LITTLE *conceals his horror imperfectly.* CUT TO *patient's room, which is full of flowers and candy boxes and books. The patient is* SYLVIA LOVEJOY, *a billionaire's widow.* SYLVIA *is no longer anything but a head connected to pipes*

*and wires coming up through the floor, but this is not
immediately apparent. The first shot of her is a* CLOSE-UP,
with GLORIA, *a gorgeous beautician, standing behind her.*
SYLVIA *is a heartbreakingly good-looking old lady, once a
famous beauty. She is crying now.*

SYLVIA: Gloria—

GLORIA: Ma'am?

SYLVIA: Wipe these tears away before somebody comes in
and sees them.

GLORIA *(wanting to cry herself):* Yes, ma'am *(She wipes
the tears away with Kleenex, studies the results) There.
There.*

SYLVIA: I don't know what came over me. Suddenly I was
so sad I couldn't stand it.

GLORIA: Everybody has to cry *sometimes.*

SYLVIA: It's passing now. Can you tell I've been crying?

GLORIA: *No. No.*

*She is unable to control her own tears anymore. She goes
to a window so* SYLVIA *can't see her cry.* CAMERA BACKS
AWAY *to reveal the tidy, clinical abomination of the head
and wires and pipes. The head is on a tripod. There is a
black box with winking colored lights hanging under the
head, where the chest would normally be. Mechanical arms
come out of the box where arms would normally be. There
is a table within easy reach of the arms. On it are a pen and
paper, a partially solved jigsaw puzzle and a bulky knitting
bag. Sticking out of the bag are needles and a sweater in
progress. Hanging over* SYLVIA*'s head is a microphone on
a boom.*

SYLVIA *(sighing):* Oh, what a *foolish* old woman
you must think I am. (GLORIA *shakes her head in de-*

nial, is unable to reply) Gloria? Are you still there?

GLORIA: Yes.

SYLVIA: Is anything the matter?

GLORIA: No.

SYLVIA: You're *such* a good friend, Gloria. I want you to know I feel that with all my heart.

GLORIA: I like you, too.

SYLVIA: If you ever have any problems I can help you with, I hope you'll ask me.

GLORIA: I will, I *will.*

HOWARD DERBY, *the hospital mail clerk, dances in with an armload of letters. He is a merry old fool.*

DERBY: Mailman! Mailman!

SYLVIA *(brightening):* Mailman! God *bless* the mailman!

DERBY: How's the patient today?

SYLVIA: Very sad a moment ago. But now that I see you, I want to sing like a bird.

DERBY: Fifty-three letters today. There's even one from Leningrad.

SYLVIA: There's a blind woman in Leningrad. Poor soul, *poor* soul.

DERBY *(making a fan of the mail, reading postmarks):* West Virginia, Honolulu, Brisbane, Australia—

SYLVIA *selects an envelope at random.*

SYLVIA: Wheeling, West Virginia. Now, who do I know in Wheeling? *(She opens the envelope expertly with her mechanical hands, reads)* "Dear Mrs. Lovejoy: You don't know me, but I just read about you in the *Reader's Digest,* and I'm sitting here with tears streaming down my cheeks." *Reader's Digest?* My goodness—that arti-

cle was printed fourteen years ago! And she just *read*
it?

DERBY: Old *Reader's Digest*s go on and on. I've got one
at home I'll bet is ten years old. I still read it every time
I need a little inspiration.

SYLVIA *(reading on):* "I am never going to complain
about anything that ever happens to me ever again. I
thought I was as unfortunate as a person can get when
my husband shot his girlfriend six months ago and then
blew his own brains out. He left me with seven children
and with eight payments still to go on a Buick Road-
master with three flat tires and a busted transmission.
After reading about you, though, I sit here and count
my blessings." Isn't that a nice letter?

DERBY: Sure is.

SYLVIA: There's a P.S.: "Get well real soon, you *hear?*"
(She puts the letter on the table) There isn't a letter from
Vermont, is there?

DERBY: Vermont?

SYLVIA: Last month, when I had that low spell, I wrote
what I'm afraid was a very stupid, self-centered, self-
pitying letter to a young doctor I read about in the
Ladies' Home Journal. I'm so ashamed. I live in fear
and trembling of what he's going to say back to me—
if he answers at all.

GLORIA: What could he say? What could he *possibly* say?

SYLVIA: He could tell me about the *real* suffering going
on out there in the world, about people who don't know
where the next meal is coming from, about people
so poor they've never *been* to a doctor in their whole
lives. And to think of all the help I've had—all the
tender, loving care, all the latest wonders science has to
offer.

CUT TO *corridor outside* SYLVIA *'s room. There is a sign on the door saying,* ALWAYS ENTER SMILING! FRANKEN-STEIN *and* LITTLE *are about to enter.*

LITTLE: She's in *there?*

FRANKENSTEIN: Every part of her that isn't downstairs.

LITTLE: And everybody obeys this sign, I'm sure.

FRANKENSTEIN: Part of the therapy. We treat the *whole* patient here.

GLORIA *comes from the room, closes the door tightly, then bursts into noisy tears.*

FRANKENSTEIN *(to* GLORIA, *disgusted):* Oh, for crying out loud. And what is this?

GLORIA: Let her *die,* Dr. Frankenstein. For the love of God, let her *die!*

LITTLE: This is her *nurse?*

FRANKENSTEIN: She hasn't got brains enough to be a nurse. She is a lousy beautician. A hundred bucks a week she makes—just to take care of one woman's face and hair. (*To* GLORIA) You blew it, honeybunch. You're through.

GLORIA: What?

FRANKENSTEIN: Pick up your check and scram.

GLORIA: I'm her closest friend.

FRANKENSTEIN: Some friend! You just asked me to knock her off.

GLORIA: In the name of mercy, yes, I did.

FRANKENSTEIN: You're that sure there's a heaven, eh? You want to send her right up there so she can get her wings and harp.

GLORIA: I know there's a hell. I've seen it. It's in there, and you're its great inventor.

FRANKENSTEIN *(stung, letting a moment pass before replying):* Christ—the things people say sometimes.

GLORIA: It's time somebody who loves her spoke up.

FRANKENSTEIN: Love.

GLORIA: You wouldn't know what that is.

FRANKENSTEIN: Love. *(More to himself than to her)* Do I have a wife? No. Do I have a mistress? No. I have loved only two women in my life—my mother and that woman in there. I wasn't able to save my mother from death. I had just graduated from medical school and my mother was dying of cancer of the everything. "OK, wise guy," I said to myself, "you're such a hot-shot doctor from Heidelberg, now, let's see you save your mother from death." And everybody told me there wasn't anything I could do for her, and I said, "I don't give a damn. I'm gonna do something anyway." And they finally decided I was nuts and they put me in a crazyhouse for a little while. When I got out, she was dead—the way all the wise men said she had to be. What those wise men didn't know was all the wonderful things machinery could do—and neither did I, but I was gonna find out. So I went to the Massachusetts Institute of Technology and I studied mechanical engineering and electrical engineering and chemical engineering for six long years. I lived in an attic. I ate two-day-old bread and the kind of cheese they put in mousetraps. When I got out of MIT, I said to myself, "OK, boy—it's just barely possible now that you're the only guy on earth with the proper education to practice 20th century medicine." I went to work for the Curley Clinic in Boston. They brought in this woman who was beautiful on the outside and a mess on the inside. She was the image of my mother. She was the widow of a man who had left her five-hundred million dollars. She didn't have any relatives. The wise men said again, "This lady's gotta die." And I said to them, "Shut up and listen. I'm gonna tell you what we're gonna do."

Silence.

LITTLE: That's—that's quite a story.

FRANKENSTEIN: It's a story about *love.* (*To* GLORIA) That love story started years and years before you were born, you great lover, you. And it's still going on.

GLORIA: Last month, she asked me to bring her a pistol so she could shoot herself.

FRANKENSTEIN: You think I don't know that? (*Jerking a thumb at* LITTLE) Last month, she wrote him a letter and said, "Bring me some cyanide, doctor, if you're a doctor with any heart at all."

LITTLE (*startled*): You *knew* that. You—you read her mail?

FRANKENSTEIN: So we'll know what she's *really* feeling. She might try to fool us sometime—just *pretend* to be happy. I told you about that bum transistor last month. We maybe wouldn't have known anything was wrong if we hadn't read her mail and listened to what she was saying to lame-brains like this one here. (*Feeling challenged*) Look—you go in there all by yourself. Stay as long as you want, ask her anything. Then you come back out and tell me the truth: Is that a happy woman in there, or is that a woman in hell?

LITTLE (*hesitating*): I—

FRANKENSTEIN: Go on in! I got some more things to say to this young lady—to Miss Mercy Killing of the Year. I'd like to show her a body that's been in a casket for a couple of years sometime—let her see how pretty death is, this thing she wants for her friend.

LITTLE *gropes for something to say, finally mimes his wish to be fair to everyone. He enters the patient's room.* CUT TO *room.* SYLVIA *is alone, faced away from the door.*

SYLVIA: Who's that?

LITTLE: A friend—somebody you wrote a letter to.

SYLVIA: That could be anybody. Can I see you, please? (LITTLE *obliges. She looks him over with growing affection.*) Dr. Little—family doctor from Vermont.

LITTLE *(bowing slightly):* Mrs. Lovejoy—how are you today?

SYLVIA: Did you bring me cyanide?

LITTLE: No.

SYLVIA: I wouldn't take it today. It's such a lovely day. I wouldn't want to miss it, or tomorrow, either. Did you come on a snow-white horse?

LITTLE: In a blue Oldsmobile.

SYLVIA: What about your patients, who love and need you so?

LITTLE: Another doctor is covering for me. I'm taking a week off.

SYLVIA: Not on my account.

LITTLE: No.

SYLVIA: Because I'm fine. You can see what wonderful hands I'm in.

LITTLE: Yes.

SYLVIA: One thing I don't need is another doctor.

LITTLE: Right.

Pause.

SYLVIA: I do wish I had somebody to talk to about death,

53

though. You've seen a lot of it, I suppose.

LITTLE: Some.

SYLVIA: And it was a blessing for some of them—when they died?

LITTLE: I've heard that said.

SYLVIA: But you don't say so yourself.

LITTLE: It's not a professional thing for a doctor to say, Mrs. Lovejoy.

SYLVIA: Why have other people said that certain deaths have been a blessing?

LITTLE: Because of the pain the patient was in, because he couldn't be cured at any price—at any price within his means. Or because the patient was a vegetable, had lost his mind and couldn't get it back.

SYLVIA: At any price.

LITTLE: As far as I know, it is not now possible to beg, borrow or steal an artificial mind for someone who's lost one. If I asked Dr. Frankenstein about it, he might tell me that it's the coming thing.

Pause.

SYLVIA: It *is* the coming thing.

LITTLE: He's told you so?

SYLVIA: I asked him yesterday what would happen if my brain started to go. He was serene. He said I wasn't to worry my pretty little head about that. "We'll cross that bridge when we come to it," he told me. *(Pause)* Oh, God, the bridges I've crossed!

CUT TO *room full of organs, as before.* SWIFT *is at the console.* FRANKENSTEIN *and* LITTLE *enter.*

FRANKENSTEIN: You've made the grand tour and now here you are back at the beginning.

LITTLE: And I still have to say what I said at the beginning: "My God—oh, my God."

FRANKENSTEIN: It's gonna be a little tough going back to the aspirin-and-laxative trade after this, eh?

LITTLE: Yes. *(Pause)* What's the cheapest thing here?

FRANKENSTEIN: The simplest thing. It's the goddamn pump.

LITTLE: What does a heart go for these days?

FRANKENSTEIN: Sixty thousand dollars. There are cheaper ones and more expensive ones. The cheap ones are junk. The expensive ones are jewelry.

LITTLE: And how many are sold a year now?

FRANKENSTEIN: Six hundred, give or take a few.

LITTLE: Give one, that's life. Take one, that's death.

FRANKENSTEIN: If the trouble is the heart. It's lucky if you have trouble that cheap. (*To* SWIFT) Hey, Tom— put her to sleep so he can see how the day ends around here.

SWIFT: It's twenty minutes ahead of time.

FRANKENSTEIN: What's the difference? We put her to sleep for twenty minutes extra, she still wakes up tomorrow feeling like a million bucks, unless we got another bum transistor.

LITTLE: Why don't you have a television camera aimed at her, so you can watch her on a screen?

FRANKENSTEIN: She didn't want one.

LITTLE: She gets what she wants?

FRANKENSTEIN: She got *that.* What the hell do we have to watch her face for? We can look at the meters down here and find out more about her than she can know about herself. (*To* SWIFT) Put her to sleep, Tom.

SWIFT (*to* LITTLE): It's just like slowing down a car or banking a furnace.

LITTLE: Um.

FRANKENSTEIN: Tom, too, has degrees in both engineering and medicine.

LITTLE: Are you tired at the end of a day, Tom?

SWIFT: It's a good kind of tiredness—as though I'd flown a big jet from New York to Honolulu, or something like that. *(Taking hold of a lever)* And now we'll bring Mrs. Lovejoy in for a happy landing. *(He pulls the lever gradually and the machinery slows down)* There.

FRANKENSTEIN: Beautiful.

LITTLE: She's asleep?

FRANKENSTEIN: Like a baby.

SWIFT: All I have to do now is wait for the night man to come on.

LITTLE: Has anybody ever brought her a suicide weapon?

FRANKENSTEIN: No. We wouldn't worry about it if they did. The arms are designed so she can't possibly point a gun at herself or get poison to her lips, no matter how she tries. That was Tom's stroke of genius.

LITTLE: Congratulations.

Alarm bell rings. Light flashes.

FRANKENSTEIN: Who could that be? (*To* LITTLE) Somebody just went into her room. We better check! (*To* SWIFT) Lock the door up there, Tom—so whoever it is, we got 'em. (SWIFT *pushes a button that locks door upstairs. To* LITTLE) You come with me.

CUT TO *patient's room.* SYLVIA *is asleep, snoring gently.* GLORIA *has just sneaked in. She looks around furtively, takes a revolver from her purse, makes sure it's loaded, then hides it in* SYLVIA's *knitting bag. She is barely finished when* FRANKENSTEIN *and* LITTLE *enter breathlessly,*

FRANKENSTEIN *opening the door with a key.*

FRANKENSTEIN: What's this?

GLORIA: I left my watch up here. *(Pointing to watch)* I've got it now.

FRANKENSTEIN: Thought I told you never to come into this building again.

GLORIA: I won't.

FRANKENSTEIN (*to* LITTLE): You keep her right there. I'm gonna check things over. Maybe there's been a little huggery buggery. (*To* GLORIA) How would you like to be in court for attempted murder, eh? *(Into microphone)* Tom? Can you hear me?

SWIFT *(voice from squawk box on wall):* I hear you.

FRANKENSTEIN: Wake her up again. I gotta give her a check.

SWIFT: Cock-a-doodle-doo.

Machinery can be heard speeding up below. SYLVIA *opens her eyes, sweetly dazed.*

SYLVIA (*to* FRANKENSTEIN): Good morning, Norbert.

FRANKENSTEIN: How do you feel?

SYLVIA: The way I always feel when I wake up—fine—vaguely at sea. Gloria! Good morning!

GLORIA: Good morning.

SYLVIA: Dr. Little! You're staying another day?

FRANKENSTEIN: It isn't morning. We'll put you back to sleep in a minute.

SYLVIA: I'm sick again?

FRANKENSTEIN: I don't think so.

SYLVIA: I'm going to have to have another operation?

FRANKENSTEIN: Calm down, calm down. *(He takes an ophthalmoscope from his pocket)*

SYLVIA: How can I be calm when I think about another operation?

FRANKENSTEIN *(into microphone):* Tom—give her some tranquilizers.

SWIFT *(squawk box):* Coming up.

SYLVIA: What else do I have to lose? My ears? My hair?

FRANKENSTEIN: You'll be calm in a minute.

SYLVIA: My eyes? My eyes, Norbert—are they going next?

FRANKENSTEIN *(to* GLORIA): Oh, boy, baby doll—will you look what you've done? *(Into microphone)* Where the hell are those tranquilizers?

SWIFT: Should be taking effect just about now.

SYLVIA: Oh, well. It doesn't matter. *(As* FRANKENSTEIN *examines her eyes)* It *is* my eyes, isn't it?

FRANKENSTEIN: It isn't your anything.

SYLVIA: Easy come, easy go.

FRANKENSTEIN: You're healthy as a horse.

SYLVIA: I'm sure somebody manufactures excellent eyes.

FRANKENSTEIN: RCA makes a damn good eye, but we aren't gonna buy one for a while yet. *(He backs away, satisfied)* Everything's all right up here. (*To* GLORIA) Lucky for you.

SYLVIA: I love it when friends of mine are lucky.

SWIFT: Put her to sleep again?

FRANKENSTEIN: Not yet. I want to check a couple of things down there.

SWIFT: Roger and out.

CUT TO LITTLE, GLORIA *and* FRANKENSTEIN *entering the machinery room minutes later.* SWIFT *is at the console.*

SWIFT: Night man's late.

FRANKENSTEIN: He's got troubles at home. You want a

58

good piece of advice, boy? Don't ever get married. *(He scrutinizes meter after meter)*

GLORIA *(appalled by her surroundings):* My God—oh, my God—

LITTLE: You've never seen this before?

GLORIA: No.

FRANKENSTEIN: She was the great hair specialist. We took care of everything else—everything but the hair. *(The reading on a meter puzzles him)* What's this? *(He socks the meter, which then gives him the proper reading)* that's more like it.

GLORIA *(emptily):* Science.

FRANKENSTEIN: What did you think it was like down here?

GLORIA: I was afraid to think. Now I can see why.

FRANKENSTEIN: You got any scientific background at all —any way of appreciating even slightly what you're seeing here?

GLORIA: I flunked earth science twice in high school.

FRANKENSTEIN: What do they teach in beauty college?

GLORIA: Dumb things for dumb people. How to paint a face. How to curl or uncurl hair. How to cut hair. How to dye hair. Fingernails. Toenails in the summertime.

FRANKENSTEIN: I suppose you're gonna crack off about this place after you get out of here—gonna tell people all the crazy stuff that goes on.

GLORIA: Maybe.

FRANKENSTEIN: Just remember this: You haven't got the brains or the education to talk about any aspect of our operation. Right?

GLORIA: Maybe.

FRANKENSTEIN: What *will* you say to the outside world?

GLORIA: Nothing very complicated—just that. . . .

FRANKENSTEIN: Yes?

GLORIA: That you have the head of a dead woman connected to a lot of machinery, and you play with it all day long, and you aren't married or anything, and that's all you do.

FREEZE SCENE *as a still photograph.* FADE TO *black.* FADE IN *same still. Figures begin to move.*

FRANKENSTEIN *(aghast):* How can you call her dead? She reads the *Ladies' Home Journal!* She talks! She knits! She writes letters to pen pals all over the world!

GLORIA: She's like some horrible fortunetelling machine in a penny arcade.

FRANKENSTEIN: I thought you loved her.

GLORIA: Every so often, I see a tiny little spark of what she used to be. I love that spark. Most people say they love her for her courage. What's that courage worth, when it comes from down here? You could turn a few faucets and switches down here and she'd be volunteering to fly a rocket ship to the moon. But no matter what you do down here, that little spark goes on thinking, "For the love of God—somebody get me out of here!"

FRANKENSTEIN *(glancing at the console):* Dr. Swift—is that microphone open?

SWIFT: Yeah. *(Snapping his fingers)* I'm sorry.

FRANKENSTEIN: Leave it open. (*To* GLORIA) She's heard every word you've said. How does that make you feel?

GLORIA: She can hear me now?

FRANKENSTEIN: Run off at the mouth some more. You're saving me a lot of trouble. Now I won't have to explain to her what sort of friend you really were and why I gave you the old heave-ho.

GLORIA *(drawing nearer to the microphone):* Mrs. Love-joy?

SWIFT *(reporting what he has heard on the headphones):* She says, "What is it, dear?"

GLORIA: There's a loaded revolver in your knitting bag, Mrs. Lovejoy—in case you don't want to live anymore.

FRANKENSTEIN *(not in the least worried about the pistol but filled with contempt and disgust for* GLORIA*):* You total imbecile. Where did you get a pistol?

GLORIA: From a mail-order house in Chicago. They had an ad in *True Romances.*

FRANKENSTEIN: They sell guns to crazy broads.

GLORIA: I could have had a bazooka if I'd wanted one. Fourteen-ninety-eight.

FRANKENSTEIN: I am going to get that pistol now and it is going to be exhibit A at your trial. *(He leaves)*

LITTLE *(to* SWIFT*):* Shouldn't you put the patient to sleep?

SWIFT: There's no way she can hurt herself.

GLORIA *(to* LITTLE*):* What does he mean?

LITTLE: Her arms are fixed so she can't point a gun at herself.

GLORIA *(sickened):* They even thought of that.

CUT TO SYLVIA's *room.* FRANKENSTEIN *is entering.* SYLVIA *is holding the pistol thoughtfully.*

FRANKENSTEIN: Nice playthings you have.

SYLVIA: You mustn't get mad at Gloria, Norbert. I asked her for this. I begged her for this.

FRANKENSTEIN: Last month.

SYLVIA: Yes.

FRANKENSTEIN: But everything is better now.

SYLVIA: Everything but the spark.

FRANKENSTEIN: Spark?

SYLVIA: The spark that Gloria says she loves—the tiny spark of what I used to be. As happy as I am right now, that spark is begging me to take this gun and put it out.

FRANKENSTEIN: And what is your reply?

SYLVIA: I am going to do it, Norbert. This is goodbye. *(She tries every which way to aim the gun at herself, fails and fails, while* FRANKENSTEIN *stands calmly by)* That's no accident, is it?

FRANKENSTEIN: We very much don't want you to hurt yourself. We love you, too.

SYLVIA: And how much longer must I live like this? I've never dared ask before.

FRANKENSTEIN: I would have to pull a figure out of a hat.

SYLVIA: Maybe you'd better not. *(Pause)* Did you pull one out of a hat?

FRANKENSTEIN: At least five hundred years.

Silence.

SYLVIA: So I will still be alive—long after you are gone?

FRANKENSTEIN: Now is the time, my dear Sylvia, to tell you something I have wanted to tell you for years. Every organ downstairs has the capacity to take care of two human beings instead of one. And the plumbing and wiring have been designed so that a second human being can be hooked up in two shakes of a lamb's tail. *(Silence)* Do you understand what I am saying to you, Sylvia? *(Silence. Passionately)* Sylvia! I will be that second human being! Talk about marriage! Talk about great love stories from the past! Your kidney will be my kidney! Your liver will be my liver! Your heart will be my heart! Your ups will be my ups and your downs will be my downs! We will live in such perfect harmony,

Sylvia, that the gods themselves will tear out their hair in envy!

SYLVIA: This is what you want?

FRANKENSTEIN: More than anything in this world.

SYLVIA: Well, then—here it is, Norbert. *(She empties the revolver into him)*

CUT TO *same room almost a half hour later. A second tripod has been set up, with* FRANKENSTEIN*'s head on top.* FRANKENSTEIN *is asleep and so is* SYLVIA. SWIFT, *with* LITTLE *standing by, is feverishly making a final connection to the machinery below. There are pipe wrenches and a blowtorch and other plumber's and electrician's tools lying around.*

SWIFT: That's gotta be it. *(He straightens up, looks around)* That's gotta be it.

LITTLE *(consulting watch):* Twenty-eight minutes since the first shot was fired.

SWIFT: Thank God you were around.

LITTLE: What you really needed was a plumber.

SWIFT *(into microphone):* Charley—we're all set up here. You all set down there?

CHARLEY *(squawk box):* All set.

SWIFT: Give 'em plenty of martinis.

GLORIA *appears numbly in doorway.*

CHARLEY: They've got 'em. They'll be higher than kites.

SWIFT: Better give 'em a touch of LSD, too.

CHARLEY: Coming up.

SWIFT: Hold it! I forgot the phonograph. (*To* LITTLE) Dr. Frankenstein said that if this ever happened, he wanted a certain record playing when he came to. He said it was in with the other records—in a plain white jacket. (*To* GLORIA) See if you can find it.

GLORIA *goes to phonograph, finds the record.*

GLORIA: This it?

SWIFT: Put it on.

GLORIA: Which side?

SWIFT: I don't know.

GLORIA: There's tape over one side.

SWIFT: The side *without* tape. (GLORIA *puts record on. Into microphone*) Stand by to wake up the patients.

CHARLEY: Standing by.

Record begins to play. It is a Jeanette MacDonald–Nelson Eddy duet, "Ah, Sweet Mystery of Life."

SWIFT *(into microphone):* Wake 'em up!

FRANKENSTEIN *and* SYLVIA *wake up, filled with formless pleasure. They dreamily appreciate the music, eventually catch sight of each other, perceive each other as old and beloved friends.*

SYLVIA: Hi, there.

FRANKENSTEIN: Hello.

SYLVIA: How do you feel?

FRANKENSTEIN: Fine. Just fine.

"There's a
Maniac
Loose
Out
There"

JACK the Ripper used to get compliments on the way he dissected the women he killed. "It is stated that some anatomical skill seems to have been displayed in the way in which the lower part of the body was mutilated," said the London *Times* of October 1, 1888.

Now Cape Cod has a mutilator. The pieces of four young women were found in February and March of this year—in shallow graves in Truro. Whoever did it was no artist with a knife. He chopped up the women with what the police guess was probably a brush hook or an ax.

It couldn't have taken too long to do.

At least two of the women, a schoolteacher and a college girl from Providence, Rhode Island, had been shot with a .22. Since the victims were cut into so many random chunks, only the murderer could make an informed guess as to what the actual causes of death might have been.

Stained rope was found at the foot of a tree near the graves. There was also rope around one of the victims' heads, and so on. The details are horrible and pitiful and sickening.

The police are sure they have the murderer. He is locked up now in the Barnstable County House of Correction—high on a hill, three blocks from here. He is a divorced Provincetown carpenter, a gentle, quiet six-footer—a twenty-four-year-old whose ex-wife, Avis, is prepared to testify that he is innocent. He married her after he got her pregnant—when she was only fourteen.

His name is Antone C. Costa. He is the father of three. "He wanted a little girl," says his wife. "He was disappointed when the first child was a boy. When the second was a boy he was really depressed. But when Nichole was born he was overjoyed. He adores Nichole."

My nineteen-year-old daughter Edith knows Tony Costa. She met him during a crazy summer she spent on her own in Provincetown, knew him well enough to receive and decline an invitation he evidently extended to many girls: "Come and see my marijuana patch."

There really was a marijuana patch for girls to see, Tony claims, a modest one—two female plants not far from the graves.

Graffiti seen recently on the wall of a Truro Laundromat: "Tony Costa digs girls."

Sick joke told recently on Cape Cod: "Tony Costa, with his mustache and long sideburns and granny glasses and dark turtleneck, walked into a Cadillac agency in Hyannis, and priced an El Dorado. 'It'll cost you an arm and a leg,' said the salesman. And Tony said, 'It's a deal.' "

An architect told me that joke. He laughed nervously afterward. And I sense that his giggling blankness in the face of horror is a reaction typical of most middle-class males on Cape Cod. The blankness is a failure to imagine why anybody would want to chop up four harmless girls.

Edmund Dinis, the district attorney who will personally present the Commonwealth's case against Costa, is troubled by this blankness too. "In this instance," he told us, "we will not attempt to establish a motive. Who knows why anybody would do such a thing?"

Mr. Dinis was interested to hear that my daughter knew the accused. "What does *she* say?" he asked. Dinis is a large, grave, earnest man who has never married. He is three years younger than I am, which makes him forty-four. He seemed bleakly open to any sort of information from young people which would allow him to understand this young people's crime.

"If Tony really is a murderer," I said, "it is a surprise to Edith. She never suspected it. Then again, she isn't very old. Up to now she has never suspected *that* much evil in anybody. She has always felt safe."

"What did *she* say—exactly," insisted Dinis. "What were *her* words?"

"She said, and this was on the telephone from Iowa City, where she goes to school now: 'If Tony is a murderer, then *anybody* could be a murderer.' This was news to her."

Mr. Dinis sat back, disappointed. What he had hoped to hear, I guess, was something enlightening about the culture of the hippies, who are so numerous in Provincetown—maybe talk about drugs.

I myself have spoken to a few young people about the Provincetown drug scene, have put this question to them: "If the person who committed the Truro murders was high on something when he killed, what drug do you think he swallowed?" I remind them how crude the butchery was, how shallow the graves were, even though it would have been easy to dig deep tombs in the woodland floor, which was sand.

The answer, invariably: "Speed."

The Truro murders may not be speed murders, and Tony Costa may not have committed them—but he has had at least one really awful trip on speed. That was in San Francisco. He thought he was going to suffocate, and passed out. So he was admitted to the emergency room of a hospital.

I found out about that from Lester Allen, one of two Cape Codders I know who are writing books about the murders. Mr. Allen is a retired newspaperman who has seen seven executions—three of them in one night. They made him ill. He has been hired by the defense lawyers, two local men, to find out all he can that will help Tony's cause. Tony and his friends and relatives have talked to him copiously. He has 1,100 pages of transcribed conversations so far.

Nowhere in all those pages, he told me, is there the slightest hint of how or why the murders were done. Nobody can imagine.

After Tony was arrested, he was sent to Bridgewater State Hospital for observation. He was polite but uncommunicative. At one point, though, he asked to see the district attorney. He wanted to ask Mr. Dinis what he was doing about the murders on Cape Cod. He said this: "There's a maniac loose out there."

Everybody closely related to the case has had some experience with drugs," Lester Allen told me, "except, of course, for the lawyers and police." He finds the culture of the young in Provincetown so different from his own that he often sounds like an anthropologist far from home —among the Kwakiutls, say, or the Yukaghir.

Among the young, Hermann Hesse is thought to be a very great writer. Authority is despised because of its cruel stupidities in pot busts and slums and Vietnam. Pot and speed and LSD are easily available close to home—or *were,* anyway, until Tony got busted for murder. Participants in the culture commonly refer to themselves as "freaks."

Here is a question a Provincetown freak put to a straight person, a diffident attempt to find out how angry the straight community might be about the chopped-up women: "Is this going to be bad for the freaks?"

Freaks are worth money to the businessman on the narrow streets of Provincetown. Thousands of tourists come in the summertime to gawk at them—and to gawk at all the shameless, happy homosexuals, and at the painters and the Portuguese fishermen too. I doubt that tourists seeing Tony around town last summer found him much of an entertainment. He was neat and clean—cleaner than almost anybody, in fact, since he took three showers a day.

Tony Costa has an ulcer, says Lester Allen.

When the bodies were found late last winter, tourists arrived off-season. Many brought kiddies and shovels and picnic lunches. They wanted to help *dig*. They were puzzled when park rangers and police and firemen found them disgusting.

Headline in the Cape Cod *Standard Times*, March 9, 1969: MORBID MAGNET DRAWS CROWDS TO TRURO GRAVES

Lester Allen assures me that an enterprising young businessman is now selling packaged sand from the grave sites for fifty cents a pound. Want some?

Here is who the pitiful victims were, in order of off-season death:

"There's a Maniac Loose Out There"

Sydney Monzon, eighteen, a local girl from Eastham, who disappeared around May 25, 1968. She was working for a Provincetown A&P, left her bike leaning against the store one day, was never seen again. Her sister thought she had gone to Europe with another girl. Bon voyage.

Susan Perry, seventeen, of Provincetown, who disappeared September 8—after Labor Day. Her parents were divorced. Her father was a fisherman. Her parents never reported her missing, assumed that she had moved to another town. Bon voyage again. Hers was the first body found. It was identified by a ring—her mother's wedding band.

Patricia Walsh and Mary Ann Wysocki, both twenty-three, both of Providence, who came to Provincetown together on Friday, January 24 of this year—in Miss Walsh's pale-blue VW bug. They were on an off-season lark. If they knew Tony, they gave no sign of it when their landlady introduced them to him after they had checked into a rooming house for five dollars a night. Off-season rates are low.

Tony, divorced for about six months, was staying there too. He helped with their luggage. Who says chivalry is dead?

And Miss Walsh and Miss Wysocki vanished. Their empty car was spotted near the marijuana patch, then the car vanished too. Then bodies were found—not two, but four.

The missing car showed up in storage in Burlington, Vermont. It had been stored by Tony Costa, so they busted him for murder.

71

Kurt Vonnegut, Jr.

Evelyn Lawson, a Hyannis friend of mine, a columnist for the *Register,* a weekly paper, is also writing a book about the murders. With the help of Provincetown's Norman Mailer, she got a contract with World Publishing. New American Library made a lot of money with *The Boston Strangler.* Tony Curtis made a lot of money out of that one too.

The Strangler was another New England specialist in killing women, as opposed to men. Women are so easy to kill—so weak and friendly, so fond of new people and places, of dates. And what *symbols* they are.

Evelyn Lawson is a witchcraft buff. She is also a Provincetown expert, an exotic métier. The village at the fingertip of the Cape seems a passionate and foreign little port to most people farther up the arm. As almost everybody knows, Cape Cod *is* shaped like a human arm. Chatham is at the elbow, Falmouth and Cataumet and Buzzards Bay are in the armpit. I live atop the biceps. The murdered women were found at the wrist.

The 100 percent American Pilgrims anchored briefly off Provincetown, did some laundry, then hastened on to Plymouth. There are now Portuguese where they did their laundry, and New Yorkers, and God-knows-what-else up there. "Many of the first settlers were pirates and mooncussers," says Evelyn. "Many were runaway witches who escaped from Salem."

Here is what she wrote in her column after the district attorney held a sensational press conference about the bodies:

> As Dinis talked . . . I felt my skin prickle in dread and disgust. The place where the bodies had been found

. . . was near an old cemetery, not far from a back dirt
crossroad, the typical traditional site for the witches'
Sabbath ceremonies. . . . Dinis indicated there was
evidence of cannibalism.

Evelyn further on described Tony Costa's being taken
off to jail, with his many friends watching.

One of the long-haired men of this group [she wrote]
got down on his knees in front of the prisoner and
reached for and kissed his manacled hands, proclaim-
ing loudly: "Tony, we love you!"

. . he kissing of the manacled hands, incidentally, didn't
really happen. Evelyn didn't see it, simply heard about it,
as did I, from everywhere. It was such a typical thing for
a freak to do, even if he didn't do it.

And the district attorney may have been stretching
facts, too, when he mentioned cannibals. He also announced that some of the hearts were missing. The next
day, the medical examiner, who should know, said the
hearts were there.

The so-called news became so loud and gruesome that
Costa's lawyers went to court about it, complained justly
of publicity ". . . fraught with images of sexual perver-
sions, mutilation, diabolic mischief and suggestions of occultism." They asked a judge to stop the mouths of the
prosecuting authorities. The judge complied.

So it is quiet now—except for a few tiny leaks.

ou can meet people in bars sometimes who want to leak
for money. Their brother-in-law knows a guard up at the

jail who sees Costa every day—and so on. If I wanted to see the official color photographs of what was left of the women, I could probably get them from somebody—if I were willing to pay.

I might even be able to buy a piece of the rope Tony tied the girls up with—*after* the trial. Business is business, after all, and always has been. There is money to be made on the fringes of famous murders. For instance: *I* am being paid.

Murder is no novelty on Cape Cod—nor are multiple murders that reek of drugs. Back in the lemonade summer of good old 1901, a nurse named Jane Toppan murdered Alden P. Davis, his wife, and his two daughters with morphine and atropine. This was in lovely Cataumet, about ten miles from here, where windmills sometimes still ground grain.

Leonard Wood, commander of the swashbuckling Rough Riders in the Spanish-American War, was vacationing there at the time. The President was McKinley, who was about to be shot. It might be argued that Jane Toppan was, in her own way, responding to the corporate greed and the militarism and the murderousness and corruption of her times. If so, she certainly responded in a great big way. She confessed not only to the Davis murders, but to twenty-seven others besides.

She died in a crazyhouse in 1938. That is surely where multiple murderers belong—in a crazyhouse.

Jane Toppan was an orphan who never could find out who her parents were. Tony Costa, on the other hand, knows all about his parents, and about shoals of other affectionate relatives. His father was a hero off New Guinea in the Second World War. He saved another sailor who was drowning. Then he banged his head on a coral outcrop and died. Tony has a newspaper clipping about this, proudly shows it around.

His father's life was insured for $10,000. Part of this treasure was put in trust for Tony by his mother, who remarried after a while. She still lives in Provincetown. When Tony was only thirteen, he was keeping books and handling business correspondence and making out the income tax for his stepfather, a mason.

How straight can you be?

Tony has an intelligence quotient of 121.

T ony and his ex-wife used to be Catholics. They aren't anymore. Avis said the other day, "We both believe in reincarnation, psychedelia, and God in nature."

She divorced him a year ago June, charging him with ". . . cruel and abusive treatment." This is a customary accusation, even among timid souls, in divorce actions in the Commonwealth.

R eporters who talk to Provincetown freaks about Tony often hear him spoken of in the past tense—as though he were long gone, would never return. They resent the gory advance publicity.

They want one thing very much for Tony: a fair trial.

Is it possible that Tony was framed? In early 1968 he did one of the most suicidal things a young drug-dabbler can do: He told the local police that so-and-so was selling dope. So-and-So was busted. There was a certain amount of tribal justice in this: So-and-so was from out of town.

But who would chop up and bury four nice girls to frame one small canary?

Tony was a spoiled little boy, one hears. He was never punished for anything.

In his closet in the rooming house where he helped Patricia Walsh and Mary Ann Wysocki with their luggage, police found a coil of stained rope.

Young women in America will continue to look for love and excitement in places that are as dangerous as hell. I salute them for their optimism and their nerve.

I remember now my own daughter's summer in Provincetown, where she was supposedly studying painting with oils. After that summer, she told me and her mother about a young man who would inform her from time to time that he wanted to kill her—and would. She didn't bother the police with this. It was a joke, she supposed—like inviting somebody to come see a marijuana patch.

When Tony was arrested, I called her up in Iowa City, and I said, "Edith—that guy who kept saying he was going to kill you: was his name Tony Costa?"

"No, no," she said. "Tony wouldn't say anything like that. Tony wasn't the one."

Then I told her about Tony Costa's arrest.

Excelsior!
We're
Going to
the Moon!
Excelsior!

My brother Bernard saw a spaceship go up one time from Cape Kennedy, and he told me: "You know, if you're right *there*, the whole thing almost seems worth it." It was *almost* a billion-dollar thrill, he said—the noise in particular.

Noise.

"Some fireworks!" he said. "The earth moved!" We are so old that we have both had extensive personal experiences with fireworks. We used to buy them from mail-order houses and stores—ladyfingers, aerial salutes, cherry bombs, nigger-chasers.

Nigger-chasers.

What my brother said about the noise at Cape Kennedy triggered this childhood response in me: "Wow!" I said. "I sure want to hear that noise."

I never have heard it, though, except from a television loudspeaker about the size of a silver dollar. I went so far as to wangle a NASA invitation to a launch, then couldn't go. But the invitation got me on a mailing list for free materials which celebrate Americans and space. The best free thing so far is a book of heavenly color photographs called *Exploring Space with a Camera*. It is on my space reference shelf next to *The Look-It-Up Book of the Stars and Planets*, by Patricia Lauber (Random House).

Look-it-up.

Miss Lauber writes for children. Here is the sort of thing she says to them:

> We are flying through space. Our craft is the earth, which orbits the sun at a speed of 67,000 miles an hour. As it orbits the sun, it spins on its axis. The sun is a star.

If I were drunk, I might cry about all that. Obviously, all Earthlings are my beloved fellow astronauts.

Beloved.

James E. Webb is less fraternal. He has nations on his mind: Some win, some lose. He says this in his foreword to *Exploring Space with a Camera:*

Excelsior! We're Going to the Moon! Excelsior!

Down through the course of history, the mastery of a new environment, or of a major new technology, or of the combination of the two as we now see in space, has had profound effects on the future of nations; on their relative strength and security; on their relations with one another; on their internal economic, social, and political affairs; and on the concepts of reality held by their people.

Their people.

He gives no examples. So I think of Germany in the First World War, learning how to fight under water. I think of Germany's amazing rockets in World War Two. I think of everybody's everything in World War Three. I think of armor and chariots and gunpowder in olden times —of floating gun platforms which gave one nation and then another one mastery of the surface of the sea.

I think of the Spaniards' mastery of the New World, with several million other Earthlings already here, with at least two other Earthling civilizations already here. I think of their masterful torture of Indians—to make the Indians tell where they had hidden gold.

Gold.

I think of white America's mastery of the South by the imaginative use of kidnapped Africans. I think of DDT.

Most of the true tales of masterfulness in new environments with new technologies have been cruel or greedy, it seems to me. The concepts of reality held by the masterful people have customarily been stupid or solipsistic in retrospect. Nobody has been remarkably secure, the masters have often ceased to be masters quickly. There have been

79

tremendous messes to be cleaned up, ravaged landscapes dotted by shattered Earthlings and their machines.

Stupid.

We have spent something like $33 billion on space so far. We should have spent it on cleaning up our filthy colonies here on earth. There is no urgency whatsoever about getting somewhere in space, much as Arthur C. Clarke wants to discover the source of the terrific radio signals coming from Jupiter. It isn't as though we aren't already going somewhere in space. Every passing hour brings the whole solar system 43,000 miles closer to Globular Cluster M13 in Hercules.

Globular Cluster M13.

Brilliant space enthusiasts like Arthur C. Clarke are treasures, of course, to the thousands of persons in the enormously profitable spaceship trade. He speaks more enchantingly than they do. His art and their commercial interests coincide. "The discovery that Jupiter is quite warm and has precisely the type of atmosphere in which life is believed to have arisen on Earth may be the prelude to the most significant biological findings of this century," he wrote recently in *Playboy*.

Playboy.

Somewhere cash registers ring.

Other innocent space boomers are scientists like Dr. Harold C. Urey and Dr. Harold Masursky and so on, men who are passionately curious to know if the craters on the moon were caused by impact or volcanic action—or both or what. They would love to know right away, if possible, and knowing *is* possible now, at fantastic expense. The money has been gathered by tax collectors, and the money has frequently been taken from American Earthlings who are poor as Job's turkey, to coin a phrase.

Job.

If all goes right with the first landing on the moon, all the Jobs in America, and all the happy people, too, will have chipped in lavishly to buy fifty pounds of rock and dust from the moon. They will also have helped an old fraternity brother of mine, who is an important man in the space program. He drives a Jaguar XKE.

XKE.

We were D.U.s together at Cornell.

D.U.s.

My fraternity brother is glowingly proud of the space program, and rightly so. (He is also proud of the fraternity, which is maybe something else again.) He is an engineer, and one night here we drank a lot of stingers, and he rhapsodized about the precision in the manufacture and launching of the "birds." And I found myself thinking of Harry Houdini, who made his living escaping from straitjackets and bank vaults and sealed chests under water.

Water.

The stingers encouraged me to suppose that Houdini, if he had had $33 billion, would have hired the best scientific minds of his time, would have had them build him a big rocket and a sort of pressure cooker in which he might ride. And he would have had them fire him at the moon.

Why would Houdini have done that? Because, even on a limited budget, he was perhaps the greatest showman of all time. He thrilled people in a way that thrills them the most: He put his life on the line. He was basically an engineer—who saved his own life again and again with strength, courage, tools, and engineering.

It is the Houdini aspects of the space program which reward most Earthlings—the dumb ones, the dropouts, the elevator operators and stenographers and so on. They are too dense ever to care about the causes of craters on the moon. Tell them about the radio signals coming from Jupiter, and they forget again right away. What they like are shows where people get killed.

Killed.

And they get them, too.

About the dumb Earthlings versus the smart Earthlings: I have known a fair number of scientists over the years, and I noticed that they were often as bored by each other's work as dumb people would be. I was a public-relations man for a while at the Research Laboratory of the General Electric Company, and I was several times privileged to see one scientist rush into the laboratory of another, ecstatic over a new piece of information. In effect, he was barking, "Eureka! Eureka! Eureka!"

Eureka.

And the scientist who had to listen to all that barking obviously couldn't wait for the visitor to shut up and go away.

I used to talk to G.E. scientists sometimes about exciting stuff I had read in *Scientific American.* I was reading it regularly in those days. I thought it was part of my job —to keep up. If the article I was discussing wasn't related to my listener's field, he would doze. I might as well have been speaking Babylonian.

So it is my guess that even our most brilliant scientists are fairly bored by the space program, unless they are directly concerned with the moon and all that. To them, too, it must look like very expensive show biz.

Eureka.

My brother is partly dependent upon the Navy for funds with which to investigate cloud physics. He was talking recently to a similarly mendicant scientist about the billions invested in space. The colleague said this, wryly: "For *that* kind of money, the least they can do is discover God."

Discover God.

You dig fifty pounds of moon rock, and what do you get? Another day older, and deeper in debt. St. Peter, don't you call me, 'cause I can't go. I owe my soul to de company sto'.

De company sto'.

Earth is such a pretty blue and pink and white pearl in the pictures NASA sent me. It looks so *clean*. You can't see all the hungry, angry Earthlings down there—and the smoke and the sewage and trash and sophisticated weaponry. I flew over Appalachia the other day—at about 500 miles an hour and five miles up. Life is said to be horrible down there in many places, but it looked like the Garden of Eden to me. I was a rich guy, way up in the sky, munching dry-roasted peanuts and sipping gin.

Eden.

"The Earth is our cradle, which we are about to leave," says Arthur C. Clarke. "And the Solar System will be our kindergarten." Most of us will never leave this cradle, of course, unless death turns out to be a form of astronautics.

There is always gin.

Gin.

I remember the apes in the great Cinerama motion picture *2001.* I remember their bloodshot eyes and their fears at night, how they learned to use tools to smash in each other's skulls. And I suppose we're not much past that on the scale of evolution, even though we now have Cinerama. The same night I saw *2001,* Dr. Nathan Pusey, president of Harvard, called the Cambridge police to his campus, and they smashed some skulls.

Cinerama.

I wonder if we really have to go out into the rest of the solar system to find kindergarten. Isn't it just barely possible that we could build one here?

Nope.

I am now reading the book *In Defense of Nature,* by the poet-naturalist John Hay (Atlantic-Little, Brown). He describes an old clammer in Maine, who will never leave the cradle:

While satellites take pictures of the earth from 25,000 miles up as it revolves through space, covered by swirling clouds, the old man sits down on a rock to rest. While laboratory minds, aided by computers, project their casual methodology into the future, he may be dreaming of the past. While science moves toward harnessing the methods of the sun through nuclear fusion and attaining unlimited energy for mankind, he stands, legs apart, head and shoulders down, intently and thoroughly digging away with his clam fork, working over the ground section by section.

Poor ape.

Good science-fiction writers of the present are not necessarily as eager as Arthur C. Clarke to found kindergartens on Jupiter, to leave the poor Maine ape and his clam rake far behind. Isaac Asimov, who is a great man, perceives three stages so far in the development of American science fiction, says we are in stage three now:

1. Adventure dominant.
2. Technology dominant.
3. Sociology dominant.

I can hope that this is a prophetic outline of Earthling history, too. I interpret "sociology" broadly—as a respectful, objective concern for the cradle natures of Earthlings on Earth.

Stage three.

In the course of an ordinary day where *I* live (Cape Cod), I never meet anyone who has the exploration of space on his mind. On a day when there has been a particularly dangerous launch, people will sometimes mention it when they meet in the post office. Otherwise, they will comment on the weather. Whatever they say in the post office is really just another way of saying "Hello."

"Hello."

If a spaceship has been aloft for some time, and has splashed down safely, my neighbors may say something like, "Thank God." They are grateful that the short-haired white athletes who went up in the pressure cooker were not killed.

Interestingly, relief is expressed if a Russian cosmonaut comes home safely, too. It would seem wrong to my neighbors if the name of a defunct Communistic spaceman were mixed into the general body count in Vietnam, were mingled willy-nilly with the encouraging news of so-and-so many Communists killed that day.

Body count.

One sacred memory from childhood is perhaps the best education," said Feodor Dostoevski. I believe that, and I hope that many Earthling children will respond to the first human footprint on the moon as a sacred thing. We need sacred things. The footprint could mean, if we let it, that Earthlings have done an unbelievably difficult and beautiful thing which the Creator, for Its own reasons, wanted Earthlings to do.

Footprint.

But that footprint will be profaned in America at once by advertising. Many profit-making corporations will congratulate themselves and their products in its name. It will come to represent, even to children, one more schlock merchandising scheme.

Merchandising scheme.

And it may be a better footprint, actually, than that. It might really *be* sacred. "Step by step," the old proverb says, "one goes a long way." Maybe the Creator really *does* want us to travel a lot more than we have traveled so far. And maybe It really does want our nervous systems to become fancier all the time. Excelsior.

Excelsior.

I prefer to think not, though, for this simple-minded reason: Earthlings who have felt that the Creator clearly wanted this or that have almost always been pigheaded and cruel. You bet.

A young American male Earthling stopped by my house the other day to talk some about a book of mine he'd read. He was the son of a Boston man who had died an alcoholic vagrant. He was on his way to Israel to find what he could find, though he wasn't a Jew. He said that his generation was the first generation to believe that it had no future. I had heard that sort of thing before.

No future.

"How can you say that," I asked him, "with the American space program going so well?"

He replied that the space program had no future, either, if the planet supporting it was being killed. That very day the papers had announced that two old Liberty ships were to be sunk in the Atlantic with tons and tons of nerve gas on board. Lake Superior, the only clean Great Lake left, was being used as a sewer for taconite waste by plants in

Duluth. The amount of carbon dioxide in the atmosphere had increased by 15 percent since the start of the Industrial Revolution, he said, and further increases would turn the planet into a vast greenhouse in which we would roast. The antiballistic missile system, he said, which would surely be built, would, in cooperation with enemy systems, and through the integrated miracles of radar, satellites, and computers, turn the planet into one glorious hair-trigger bomb.

Bomb.

"If you really *believe* these terrible things about your planet," I said, "how can you keep on living?"

"Day by day," he said. "I travel. I read." He had no girl with him, no Eve.

No Eve.

I asked him what he was reading, and he took a book out of his rucksack. It was *Music of the Spheres,* by Guy Murchie (Houghton Mifflin, 1961). I already knew the book some. I had lifted a comment Murchie made about time for a book of my own:

> I sometimes wonder whether humanity has missed the real point in raising the issue of mortality and immortality—in other words, whether mortality itself may be a finite illusion, being actually immortality and, even though constructed of just a few "years," that those few years are all the time there really is, so that, in fact, they can never cease.

I asked my visitor to show me a passage he had found to admire in the book. This was it:

> Is there nothing then but illusory space-time between us and Kingdom Come? Naturally, I cannot reach

out and touch it with my hand, but I can imagine it some way with my mind and feel its potentiality in my heart. And I can see beauty and order there—and most especially the elements of music. I can hear, in a real sense, the music of the spheres.

Address to the American Physical Society*

MY only brother is a cloud physicist. He is nine years older than I am, and was an inspiration to me in my youth. He used to work with the research laboratory of the General Electric Company in Schenectady. Back in his Schenectady days, Bernard was working with Irving Langmuir and Vincent Schaeffer on precipitating certain kinds of clouds as snow

*New York City, 1969

or rain—with dry ice or silver iodide, and maybe some other stuff.

He was notorious in Schenectady for having a horrendously messy laboratory. There was a safety officer in the laboratory who called on him regularly, begging him to clean up the death traps all around the room. One day my brother said to him, "If you think this is a mess, you should see what it's like up here." And my brother pointed to his own head. I loved him for that. We love each other very much, even though I am a humanist and he is a physicist.

I am charmed that you should call me in your program notes here a humanist. I have always thought of myself as a paranoid, as an overreactor, and a person who makes a questionable living with his mental diseases. Fiction writers are not customarily persons in the best of mental health.

Many of you are physics teachers. I have been a teacher, too. I have taught creative writing. I often wondered what I thought I was doing, teaching creative writing, since the demand for creative writers is very small in this vale of tears. I was perplexed as to what the usefulness of any of the arts might be, with the possible exception of interior decoration. The most positive notion I could come up with was what I call the canary-in-the-coal-mine theory of the arts. This theory argues that artists are useful to society because they are so sensitive. They are supersensitive. They keel over like canaries in coal mines filled with poison gas, long before more robust types realize that any danger is there.

The most useful thing I could do before this meeting today is to keel over. On the other hand, artists are keeling over by the thousands every day and nobody seems to pay the least attention.

If you want an outside opinion on your profession, you hired the wrong man. I've had the same formal education you people have had, more or less. I was a chemistry major in college. H. L. Mencken started out as a chemist. H. G. Wells did, too. My father said he would help to pay for my college education only if I studied something serious. This was in the late Thirties. *Reader's Digest* magazine was in those days celebrating the wonderful things Germans were doing with chemicals. Chemistry was obviously the coming thing. So was German. So I went to Cornell University, and I studied chemistry and German.

Actually, it was very lucky for me as a writer that I studied the physical sciences rather than English. I wrote for my own amusement. There was no kindly English professor to tell me for my own good how awful my writing really was. And there was no professor with the power to order me what to read, either. So reading and writing have been pure pleasure for me. I only read *Madame Bovary* last year. It's a very good book. I had heard that it was.

Back in my days as a chemistry student I used to be quite a technocrat. I used to believe that scientists would corner God and photograph Him in Technicolor by 1951. I used to mock my fraternity brothers at Cornell who were wasting their energies on insubstantial subjects such as sociology and government and history. And literature. I told them that all power in the future would rest properly in the hands of chemists and physicists and engineers. The fraternity brothers knew more about the future and about the uses of power than I did. They are rich and they are powerful now. They all became lawyers.

You have summoned me here in my sunset years as a writer. I am forty-six. F. Scott Fitzgerald was dead when he was my age. So was Anton Chekhov. So was D. H. Lawrence. So was George Orwell, a man I admire almost more than any other man. Physicists live longer than writers, by and large. Copernicus died at seventy. Galileo died at seventy-eight. Isaac Newton died at eighty-five. They lived that long even before the discovery of all the miracles of modern medicine. Think of how much longer they might have lived with heart transplants.

You have called me a humanist, and I have looked into humanism some, and I have found that a humanist is a person who is tremendously interested in human beings. My dog is a humanist. His name is Sandy. He is a sheep dog. I know that Sandy is a dud name for a sheep dog, but there it is.

One day when I was a teacher of creative writing at the University of Iowa, in Iowa City, I realized that Sandy had never seen a truly large carnivore. He had never smelled one, either. I assumed that he would be thrilled out of his wits. So I took him to a small zoo they had in Iowa City to see two black bears in a cage.

"Hey, Sandy," I said to him on the way to the zoo, "wait till you see. Wait till you smell."

Those bears didn't interest him at all, even though they were only three inches away. The stink was enough to knock me over. But Sandy didn't seem to notice. He was too busy watching people.

Most people are mainly interested in people, too. Or

that has been my experience in the writing game. That's why it was so intelligent of us to send human beings to the moon instead of instruments. Most people aren't very interested in instruments. One of the things that I tell beginning writers is this: "If you describe a landscape, or a cityscape, or a seascape, always be sure to put a human figure somewhere in the scene. Why? Because readers are human beings, mostly interested in human beings. People are humanists. *Most* of them are humanists, that is."

Shortly before coming to this meeting from Cape Cod, I received this letter:

> Dear Mr. Vonnegut,
>
> I saw with interest the announcement of the talk entitled "The Virtuous Scientist," to be delivered by you and Eames and Drexler at the New York A.P.S. meeting. Unfortunately, I will not be present at the New York meeting this year. However, as a humanistic physicist, I would very much appreciate receiving a copy of the talk. Thanking you in advance.
>
> *Sincerely,*
> GEORGE F. NORWOOD, JR.,
> assistant professor of physics,
> University of Miami,
> Coral Gables, Florida.

If Professor Norwood really is a humanistic physicist, then he is exactly my idea of what a virtuous physicist should be. A virtuous physicist is a humanistic physicist. Being a humanistic physicist, incidentally, is a good way to get *two* Nobel Prizes instead of one. What does a humanistic physicist do? Why, he watches people, listens to them, thinks about them, wishes them and their planet well. He wouldn't knowingly hurt people. He wouldn't knowingly help politicians or soldiers hurt people. If he comes across a technique that would obviously hurt people, he keeps it to himself. He knows that a scientist can be an accessory to murder most foul. That's simple enough, surely. That's surely clear.

I was invited here, I think, mostly because of a book of mine called *Cat's Cradle*. It is still in print, so if you rush out to buy it, you will not be disappointed. It is about an old-fashioned scientist who isn't interested in people. In the midst of a terrible family argument, he asks a question about turtles. Nobody has been talking about turtles. But the old man suddenly wants to know: When turtles pull in their heads, do their spines buckle or contract?

This absentminded old man, who doesn't give a damn for people, discovers a form of ice which is stable at room temperature. He dies, and some idiots get possession of the substance, which I call Ice-9. The idiots eventually drop some of the stuff into the sea, and the waters of the earth freeze—and that is the end of life on earth as we know it.

I got this lovely idea while I was working as a public-relations man at General Electric. I used to write publicity releases about the research laboratory there, where my brother worked. While there, I heard a story about a visit H. G. Wells had made to the laboratory in the early Thirties.

General Electric was alarmed by the news of his coming, because they did not know how to entertain him. The company told Irving Langmuir, who was a most important man in Schenectady, the only Nobel Prize winner in private industry, that he was going to have to entertain Wells. Langmuir didn't want to do it, but he dutifully tried to imagine diversions that would delight Mr. Wells. He made up a science-fiction story he hoped Mr. Wells would want to write. It was about a form of ice which was stable at room temperature. Mr. Wells was not stimulated by the story. He later died, and so did Langmuir. After Langmuir died, I thought to myself, well, I think maybe I'll write a story.

While I was writing that story about Ice-9, I happened to go to a cocktail party where I was introduced to a crystallographer. I told him about this ice which was stable at room temperature. He put his cocktail glass on the mantelpiece. He sat down in an easy chair in the corner. He did not speak to anyone or change expression for half an hour. Then he got up, came back over to the mantelpiece, and picked up his cocktail glass, and he said to me, "Nope." Ice-9 was impossible.

Be that as it may, other scientific developments have been almost that horrible. The idea of Ice-9 had a certain moral validity at any rate, even though scientifically it had to be pure bunk.

I have already called the fictitious inventor of the fictitious Ice-9 an old-fashioned sort of scientist. There used to be a lot of morally innocent scientists like him. No more. Younger scientists are extremely sensitive to the moral implications of all they do. My fictitious old-time scientist asked, among other things, this question: "What is sin?" He asked that question mockingly as though the concept of sin were as obsolete as plate armor. Young scientists, it seems to me, are fascinated by the idea of sin.

They perceive it as anything human that seriously threatens the planet and the life thereon.

While I was working at General Electric, long after the Second World War, the older scientists were generally serene, but the younger ones were frequently upset. The young ones were eager to discuss the question as to whether the atomic bomb, for instance, was a sin or not.

David Lilienthal, the first chairman of the Atomic Energy Commission, said he was going to resign his job in order to speak freely, and scientists at General Electric banded together to ask Lilienthal to come to Schenectady to speak to them. They wanted to hear what he had to say about the bomb, now that he was free to say what he pleased. Lilienthal accepted. The young scientists hired a movie theater. It was jammed the night when Lilienthal agreed to speak so freely, to gush.

The audience was silent and thrilled and frightened and awed and hopeful. Lilienthal's opening statement, as I recall it, was this: "First of all, let me say that I see no point in wallowing in misery." Then he told the scientists and their wives, their young wives, about all the wonderful benefits that peacetime uses of atomic energy were going to bring. He told about a ball bearing which was coated with a radioactive isotope and then rolled down a trough. Thanks to atomic energy, minute measurements of the wear and tear on both the ball bearing and the trough could be made.

He told, too, about his egg man, who had a malignant throat tumor the size and shape of a summer squash. This man, who was about to die, was urged to drink an atomic cocktail. The tumor disappeared entirely in a matter of days. The egg man died anyway. But Lilienthal and others like him found the experiment encouraging in the extreme.

Address to the American Physical Society

I have never seen a more depressed audience leaving a theater. *The Diary of Anne Frank* was a lighthearted comedy when compared with Lilienthal's performance for that particular audience, on that particular night, in that particular city, where science was king. The young scientists and their young wives had learned something which most scientists now realize: that their bosses are not necessarily sensitive or moral or imaginative men. Ask Wernher Von Braun. His boss had him firing rockets at London.

The old-fashioned scientist I described in *Cat's Cradle* was the product of a great depression and of World War Two and some other things, of course. The mood of technical people in World War Two can be expressed in slogans such as "Can Do!" and "The difficult we do right away; the impossible takes a little longer!"

The Second World War was a war against pure evil. I mean that seriously. There was never any need to moralize. Nothing was too horrible to do to any enemy that vile. This moral certainty and the heartlessness it encouraged did not necessarily subside when the war was won. Virtuous scientists, however, stopped saying "Can do!"

I don't find this particularly congenial, moralizing up here. Moralizing hasn't really been my style up to now. But people, university people in particular, seem to be demanding more and more that persons who lecture to them put morals at the end of their lectures.

One of the greatest public-speaking failures of my career took place last summer at Valparaiso University in Indiana, where I addressed a convention of editors of college newspapers. I said many screamingly funny things, but the applause was dismal at the end. During the evening I asked one of my hosts in what way I had offended the audience. He replied that they had hoped I would moralize. They had hired me as a moralist.

So now when I speak to students, I do moralize. I tell them not to take more than they need, not to be greedy. I tell them not to kill, even in self-defense. I tell them not to pollute water or the atmosphere. I tell them not to raid the public treasury. I tell them not to work for people who pollute water or the atmosphere, or who raid the public treasury. I tell them not to commit war crimes or to help others to commit war crimes. These morals go over very well. They are, of course, echoes of what the young say to themselves.

I had a friend from Schenectady visit me recently, and he asked me this, "Why are fewer and fewer young Americans going into science each year?" I told him that the young were impressed by the war crimes trials at Nuremberg. They were afraid that careers in science could all too easily lead to the commission of war crimes. They don't want to work on the development of new weapons. They don't want to make discoveries which will lead to improved weapons. They don't want to work for corporations that pollute water or atmosphere or raid the public treasury. So they go into other fields. They become physicists who are so virtuous that they don't go into physics at all.

At the University of Michigan, at Ann Arbor, the students have been raising hell about the university doing secret Government work. I got to talking to some of the students about the protests that have been made against the recruiters for Dow Chemical, manufacturers of napalm among other things. I offered the opinion that an attack on a Dow recruiter was about as significant as an attack on the doorman or theater usher. I didn't think the recruiter stood for anything.

I called attention to the fact that during the Dow protest at Harvard a couple of years back, the actual inventor of napalm was able to circulate through the crowd of protestors unmolested. I didn't find the fact that he was unmolested reprehensible. I saw it as a moral curiosity, though I did not mean to suggest to students at Ann Arbor that the inventor of napalm should have been given one hell of a time. I wasn't sure what I thought.

The next day I received a letter which said this:

> Dear Mr. Vonnegut,
> I heard you talk at the Canterbury house yesterday, and I must admit that I was struck by your question about Louis Fieser, who was allowed to wander unmolested through the Dow demonstration at Harvard. Your question about why students don't protest the scientists who invent weapons is valid and troublesome. I can only answer that I think we should. But do you know Louis Fieser? I don't know him personally, but I was at Harvard until this year and I have heard the old man lecture in organic chemistry. From this limited exposure and from the response of others to him in his late years, I can only suspect that a protest would be lost on him. He is a very funny and lovable man in the lecture room. I don't imagine he would understand a protest. And his personality leaves an imprint that makes it hard to use him as a symbol. In contrast, Dow representatives are such nicely impersonal representative products of the system that they are easy to protest against both immediately and symbolically.

There ends the letter.

This letter helped me to see that Dr. Fieser and other old-fashioned scientists like him were and are as innocent as Adam and Eve. There was nothing at all sinful in Dr. Fieser's creation of napalm. Scientists will never be so innocent again. Any young scientist, by contrast, when asked by the military to create a terror weapon on the order of napalm, is bound to suspect that he may be committing modern sin. God bless him for that.

Good
Missiles,
Good
Manners,
Good Night

I WENT to high school in Indianapolis with a nice girl named Barbara Masters. Her father was an eye doctor in our town. She is now the wife of our Secretary of Defense.

I was having lunch in Indianapolis recently with another man who had known her in school. He had an upper-class Hoosier accent, which sounds like a bandsaw cutting galvanized tin. He said this: "When you get to be our age, you all of a sudden realize that you are being ruled by people you went to high school with."

He was uncomfortably silent for a moment, then he said: "You all of a sudden catch on that life is nothing *but* high school. You make a fool of yourself in high school, then you go to college and learn how you should have acted in high school, and then you get out into real life, and that turns out to be high school all over again—class officers, cheerleaders, and all.

"Richard M. Nixon," he went on. There was another silence. We had no trouble imagining that we had gone to school with Mr. Nixon, too.

"So optimistic, so blooming with mental health," I said.

I live on Cape Cod now, and, on my way home from Indianapolis, I read an article by Dr. Ernest J. Sternglass in the September *Esquire*. Dr. Sternglass, a professor of radiation physics at the University of Pittsburgh, promised that, if Mr. Laird's and Mr. Nixon's Safeguard Antimissile system was ever used, all children born after that (anywhere) would die of birth defects before they could grow up and reproduce.

So I marveled again at the cheerfulness of our leaders, guys my age. They were calling for nothing less than the construction of a doomsday machine, but they went on smiling. Everything was OK.

Mr. and Mrs. Laird and I graduated from high school in 1940, incidentally. That was when we got to see the first obituaries of ourselves—in our yearbooks.

At a party a few months ago, a Hoosier friend told me that Mrs. Laird read my books and liked them. She had supposedly said that I was to get in touch with her, if I was ever in Washington, D.C. That seemed wild to me. I was a pacifist. I thought most American weapons were cruelly ridiculous. My newest book was about utterly pitiful things that happened to unarmed human beings on the ground when our bombers went about their technical duties in the sky.

But then I remembered high school, where all of us learned to respect each other's opinions—no matter what the opinions were. We learned how to be unfailingly friendly—to smile. So, maybe, the Secretary of Defense would be friendly about my pacifism and all that, and I would be expected to be friendly about the end of the world and all that.

As it happened, I found myself in Washington last June, so I left a friendly message for Mrs. Laird at her husband's office in the Pentagon. "I will be at the Sheraton Park for three days," I said. There was no reply. Maybe Mrs. Laird's supposed enthusiasm for my work was a hoax.

Word of honor—if I had been invited into the Laird home, I would have smiled and smiled. I would have understood that the defense establishment was only doing what it had to do, no matter how suicidally. I would have agreed, hearing the other fellow's side of the story, that even for planets there are worse things than death. Upon leaving, I would have thanked the Lairds for a nice time. I would have said, "I only regret that my wife couldn't have been here, too. She would have loved it."

I would have thanked God, too, that no members of the younger generation were along. Kids don't learn nice manners in high school anymore. If they met a person who was in favor of building a device which would cripple and finally kill all children everywhere, they wouldn't smile. They would bristle with hatred, which is rude.

Why
They
Read
Hesse

HERE are the bare bones of a tale that will always be popular with the young anywhere: A man travels a lot, is often alone. Money is not a serious problem. He seeks spiritual comfort, and avoids marriage and boring work. He is more intelligent than his parents and most of the people he meets. Women like him. So do poor people. So do wise old men. He experiments with sex, finds it nice but not tremendous. He encounters many queerly lovely hints that spiritual comfort really can be found. The world is beautiful. There is magic around.

The story has everything but novelty. Chrétien de

Troyes had success with it eight hundred years ago, in *Perceval le Gallois*. He had Perceval hunt for the Holy Grail, the cup Christ used at the Last Supper. Jack Kerouac and J. D. Salinger and Saul Bellow, among others, have been admired in recent times for their tales of quests.

But the modern man who told it best was Hermann Hesse. He has been dead for eight years now. He was about my father's age. He was a German, and later a Swiss. He is deeply loved by those among the American young who are questing.

His simplest, clearest, most innocent tale of seeking and finding is *Siddhartha* (1922). How popular is it? Nearly one million copies have been printed in America since 1957. One quarter of those were sold last year. This year is expected to be even better.

Hesse is no black humorist. Black humorists' holy wanderers find nothing but junk and lies and idiocy wherever they go. A chewing-gum wrapper or a used condom is often the best they can do for a Holy Grail. Not so with the wanderers of Hesse; they always find something satisfying—holiness, wisdom, hope. Here are some Hesse endings to enjoy:

> Perhaps . . . I will turn out to be a poet after all. This would mean as much, or perhaps more, to me than being a village councilor—or the builder of the stone dams. Yet it could never mean as much to me . . . as the memory of all those beloved people, from slender Rösi Girtanner to poor Boppi. (*Peter Camenzind,* 1904)

> Govinda bowed low. Incontrollable tears trickled down his old face. He was overwhelmed by a feeling of great love, of the most humble veneration. He

bowed low, right down to the ground, in front of the man sitting there motionless, whose smile reminded him of everything that he had ever loved in his life, of everything that had ever been of value and holy in his life. *(Siddhartha)*

I understood it all. I understood Pablo. I understood Mozart, and somewhere behind me I heard his ghastly laughter. I knew that all the hundred thousand pieces of life's game were in my pocket. A glimpse of its meaning had stirred my reason, and I was determined to begin the game afresh. . . . One day I would be a better hand at the game. One day I would learn how to laugh. Pablo was waiting for me, and Mozart, too. *(Steppenwolf,* 1927)

Dressing the wound hurt. Everything that has happened to me since has hurt. But sometimes when I find the key and climb deep into myself where the images of fate lie aslumber in the dark mirror, I need only bend over that dark mirror to behold my own image, now completely resembling him, my brother, my master. *(Demian,* 1925)

Lovely. Hesse has had sensitive, truly bilingual English translators, by the way—Michael Roloff and Hilda Rosner and Ursule Molinaro among them.

So an easy explanation of American youth's love for Hesse is this: He is clear and direct and well translated, and he offers hope and romance, which the young play hell finding anywhere else these days. And that is such a *sunny* explanation.

But there are darker, deeper explanations to be found —and the clue that they exist is that the most important

Hesse book to the American young, by their own account, is the wholly Germanic, hopelessly dated jumble called *Steppenwolf.*

Students of the famous Generation Gap might ponder this: Two of the leading characters in *Steppenwolf* are Johann Wolfgang von Goethe (1749–1832) and Wolfgang Amadeus Mozart (1756–1791), who appear as ghosts in dreams.

And here is a sample of dated dialogue, which the young do not choose to laugh at:

The lonely hero, Harry Haller, has picked up a girl in a dance hall, and she says, "Now we'll go and give your shoes and trousers a brush and then you'll dance the shimmy with me."

And he replies, "I can dance no shimmy, nor waltz, nor polka, nor any of the rest of them."

The mere title *Steppenwolf* (a wolf of the steppes) has magic. I can see a lonesome freshman, coming from a gas-station community to a great university, can see him roaming the big bookstore for the first time. He leaves with a small paper bag containing the first serious book he has ever bought for himself: hey presto! *Steppenwolf!*

He has nice clothes and a little money, but he is depressed and leery of women. When he reads *Steppenwolf* in his dismal room, so far from home and Mother, he will find that it is about a middle-aged man in a dismal room, far from home and Mother. This man has nice clothes and a little money, but he is depressed and leery of women.

I recently asked a young drummer, a dropout from the University of Iowa and an admirer of *Steppenwolf,* why he thought the book was selling so well. I told him an astonishing fact: Bantam Books brought out a dollar-and-a-quarter edition of *Steppenwolf* in September of last year and sold 360,000 copies in thirty days.

The drummer said that most college people were experimenting with drugs and that *Steppenwolf* harmonized perfectly with their experiences.

"I thought the best part of the drug experience was that *everything* harmonized with it—everything but the police department," I said.

The drummer admitted this was so.

I suggested to him that America teemed with people who were homesick in bittersweet ways, and that *Steppenwolf* was the most profound book about homesickness ever written.

Characters in *Steppenwolf* do use drugs from time to time, it's true—a pinch of laudanum (tincture of opium) or a sniff of cocaine now and then to chase the blues. A jazz musician gives the hero a yellow cigarette that induces fantastic dreams. But the drugs are never adored, or feared either. They are simply medicines that friends pass around. Nobody is hooked, and nobody argues that drugs are the key to anything important.

Nor have I found Hesse to be tantalized by the drug experience in his other books. He is more concerned with alcohol. Again and again, his holy wanderers love wine too much. They do something about it, too. They resolve to keep out of taverns, though they miss the uncritical companionship they've had there.

The politics espoused by the hero of *Steppenwolf* coincide with those of the American young, all right: He is against war. He hates armament manufacturers and superpatriots. No nations or political figures or historical events are investigated or praised or blamed. There are no daring schemes, no calls to action, nothing to make a radical's heart beat faster.

Hesse shocks and thrills the American young by taking them on a lunatic's tour of a splendid nightmare—down endless corridors, through halls of breaking mirrors, to costume balls, to empty theaters showing grotesque plays and films, to a wall with a thousand doors in it, and on and on. A sign appears once in an alley, fades forever. Sinister strangers hand the hero curious messages. And on and on.

A magic theater fantasy in which Harry Haller takes part proves, incidentally, that Hesse might have been one of the most screamingly funny men of his time. It may be that he was so anguished as he wrote *Steppenwolf* that his soul could get relief only by erupting into Charlie Chaplin comedy. The fantasy is about two men who climb a tree by a road. They have a rifle. They declare war on all automobiles and shoot them as they come by.

I laughed. There aren't many laughs in the works of Hermann Hesse. This is because romances work only if all the characters take life very seriously.

Steppenwolf is a Hesse freak for including a comedy— and a freak again for acknowledging modern technology and hating it, by and large. Most of his tales take place in villages and countrysides, often before the First World War. No internal-combustion engine ever shatters the silence. No telephone rings. No news comes from a radio. Messages are delivered by hand, or in the voices of a river or a wind.

Nobody in *Steppenwolf* has a telephone, although the cast is in a rich city after the war, where people do the shimmy to jazz. The hero has no radio in his room, despite his swooning loneliness, but there are radios around, because he dreams of listening to one in the company of Mozart. The Concerto Grosso in F major, by Handel, is being broadcast from Munich. The hero says this about it, marvelously: "The devilish tin trumpet spat out, without more ado, a mixture of bronchial slime and chewed rubber; that noise that owners of gramophones and radios have agreed to call music."

I have said that Hesse was about the same age as my father. My father wasn't a European, but part of his education took place in Strasbourg—before the First World War. And when I got to know him, when Hesse was writing *Steppenwolf,* my father, too, was cursing radios and films, was dreaming of Mozart and Goethe, was itching to pot-shot automobiles.

Curiously, Hesse, a man who spoke for my father's generation, is now heard loud and clear by my daughters and sons.

And I say again: What my daughters and sons are responding to in *Steppenwolf* is the homesickness of the author. I do not mock homesickness as a silly affliction that is soon outgrown. I never outgrew it and neither did my father and neither did Hesse. I miss my Mommy and Daddy, and I always will—because they were so nice to me. Now and then, I would like to be a child again.

And who am I when I spend a night alone in a motel outside, say, Erie, Pennsylvania? Who am I when I prowl that room, find only trash on television, when I search the phone book for nonexistent friends and relatives in Erie? Who am I when I think of going to a cocktail lounge for the easy comradeship there, when I imagine meeting a friendly woman out there and dread the kind of woman

I would be likely to meet? I am Steppenwolf.

The man who calls himself Steppenwolf, by the way, is one of the least carnivorous characters in fiction. He is a fool and a prig and a coward. He is a lamb.

Hesse's German parents hoped, when he was a boy, that he would become a minister. But he suffered a severe religious crisis when he was fourteen. He ran away from the seminary, tried suicide by and by. In *Beneath the Wheel* (1906), the only Hesse book I've read that has a hopelessly unhappy ending, he shows himself as an abused schoolboy who gets drunk and drowns.

He published his first book, *Peter Camenzind,* when he was twenty-seven. It was extremely popular in Germany. Hesse continued to prosper in his native land, and then, in 1912 when he was thirty-five, he left Germany forever. He eventually went to Switzerland.

He removed himself from Kaiser Wilhelm's shrill militarism, avoided Hitler, two lost world wars, the partitioning of Germany, and all that. And all that. While his former countrymen were dying and killing in the trenches, Hermann Hesse was being psychoanalyzed by Carl Jung in a multilingual peaceful little land. He published romantic novels and poetry, traveled to the Far East. He was married three times.

In 1946, one year after the death of Hitler, he received the Goethe Prize. He won a Nobel Prize a year after that —not as a German but as a Swiss. He wasn't representing a German culture that was rising from the ashes. He was representing a culture that had cleared the hell out of Germany just before the holocaust began.

This is something a lot of young Americans are considering, too—clearing out before a holocaust begins. Much luck to them. Their problem is this: The next holocaust will leave this planet uninhabitable, and the Moon is no Switzerland. Neither is Venus. Neither is Mars. In all the rest of the solar system, there is nothing to breathe. Not only would *Steppenwolf* be homesick on some other planet. He would die.

Oversexed
in
Indianapolis *

DAN Wakefield is a
friend of mine. We both went to Shortridge High School
in Indianapolis—where the students put out a *daily* paper,
by the way. His publisher is my publisher. He has boomed
my books. So I would praise his first novel, even if it were
putrid. But I wouldn't give my Word of Honor that it was
good.

Word of Honor: Mr. Wakefield has been a careful and
deep author of nonfiction for years—*Island in the City,
Revolt in the South, The Addict. . . . The Atlantic Monthly*
gave him an issue all his own for *Supernation at Peace and
War.* Word of Honor: He is also an important novelist
now.

*Review of Going All the Way *by Dan Wakefield*

Kurt Vonnegut, Jr.

Going All the Way is about what hell it is to be over-sexed in Indianapolis, and why so many oversexed people run away from there. It is also about the narrowness and dimness of many lives out that way. And I guarantee you this: Wakefield himself, having written this book, can never go home again. From now on, he will have to watch the 500-mile Speedway race on television.

This is a richer book than *Portnoy's Complaint,* with wider concerns and more intricate characters, but the sexual problems are much the same. Wakefield shows us two horny young Hoosiers, and it is easy to imagine their meeting Alexander Portnoy in a Howard Johnson's—midway between Indianapolis and New York. If they were candid with one another, they would admit that they were rotten lovers, and they might suppose mournfully that rotten lovers were not welcomed by women *anywhere.*

Going All the Way is a period piece, incidentally—set in ancient times, at the close of the Korean War. And every book is a period piece now—since years or even weeks in America no longer resemble each other at all.

This book is full of belly laughs, but I am suspicious of belly laughs as entirely happy experiences. The only way to get a belly laugh, I've found, is to undermine a surface joke with more unhappiness than most mortals can bear.

After a series of low-comedy sexual failures, for instance, one of Wakefield's heroes cuts his wrists lightly with a razor blade, ". . . so that rivulets of blood began to flow together, forming a thick little puddle." This isn't funny, and the scene becomes less funny as it goes on.

He started smearing the blood over his face and over the front of his torn shirt, like an Indian painting himself to prepare for a ceremony—a battle, a blessing, a death.

So much for sexual comedy. Nobody dies in the book, but a lot of people would like to, or at least wouldn't mind.

Wakefield's reportage of life in Middle America, as one might expect, is gruesomely accurate and enchanting. His sex-addled fools tool their parents' automobiles through a vast pinball machine whose bumpers and kickers are strip joints and taverns and gas stations and golf driving ranges and hamburger stands. They seek whorehouses, which, it turns out, have been closed for years.

They return home periodically to their smug and vapid parents, grumpily declining to say where they've been. Their stomachs, already churning with hamburgers and beer, twist even more grotesquely when their parents want to know when they are going to settle down to nice jobs and nice wives and nice houses in Indianapolis.

Finally—there is a tremendous automobile crash.

And, finally again, this wildly sexy novel isn't a sex novel. It is really about a society so drab that sex seems to the young to be the only adventure with any magic in it. When sex turns out to be merely sex, the young flee to more of the same elsewhere—and they play dangerous games with, among other things, automobiles and razor blades.

How old are Wakefield's protagonists? About the same age Ernest Hemingway was when he returned to Middle America as a quiet, wounded, authentic hero of World War One.

The Mysterious Madame Blavatsky

ADAME Helena Petrovna Blavatsky (1831–1891) was a mannish, aggressively celibate Russian noblewoman who became a United States citizen at the age of forty-seven, after she had been here five years. She did this in order to make her theories about occult matters more acceptable in America.

> The workings of my original destiny have forced me into this naturalization [she wrote to an aunt], but to my utter astonishment and disgust I was compelled to repeat publicly after the judge, like a mere parrot, the following tirade: that I would renounce forever

and even to my death every kind of submission and obedience to the Emperor of Russia.

A reporter asked her if she was married. "Married?" she said. "No. I am a widow, a blessed widow, and I thank God! I wouldn't be a slave to God Himself, let alone man."

Here is how she looked to a young female admirer in New York City in 1873:

> ... like a magnet, powerful enough to draw round her everyone who could possibly come. I saw her, day by day, sitting there rolling her cigarettes and smoking incessantly. She had a conspicuous tobacco pouch, the head of some furbearing animal, which she wore round the neck. ... I think she must have been taller than she looked, she was so broad. She had a broad face and broad shoulders. Her hair was lightish brown and crinkled.

Madame was living in a tough neighborhood because she was broke. She was often broke. Money bored her, I think. She showed her visitor a knife she had concealed in the folds of her dress, said she had *that* for any man who molested her.

Her followers liked to call her "H.P.B." Her closest friends called her "Jack," too, and she sometimes signed her letters this way.

This is *such* a pre-Freudian tale.

Madame Blavatsky has plenty of followers still. Her most important contribution to American intellectual history is this, it seems to me: She encouraged a lot of Yankees to suspect that spooky aspects of foreign religions might not be the claptrap scientists said they were.

She claimed to have traveled around the world three times before stopping off here.

> This lady [said the New York *Daily Graphic*] has led a very eventful life, travelling in most of the lands of the Orient, searching for antiquities at the base of the Pyramids, witnessing the mysteries of Hindu temples, and pushing with an armed escort far into the interior of Africa. The adventures she has encountered, the strange people she has seen, the perils by land and sea she has passed through, would make one of the most romantic stories ever told by a biographer.

She was as full of florid tales as Marco Polo. Some of them may have been fanciful.

Many Americans, I find, are dimly aware that there was a Madame Blavatsky somewhere in our P. T. Barnum past. When I make them guess who she was and what she did, they commonly suppose that she was an outstanding quack among many quacks who pretended to talk to the dead. This response is ignorant and unfair.

It was Americans who tried to turn Madame Blavatsky into a spiritualist, and she resisted them—not the other way around. This country was ghost-crazy long before she got here. The craze started in Hydeville, New York, in 1848, when three sisters, Margaret, Catharine, and Leah Fox, persuaded their neighbors that spirits were making their furniture dance. The furniture tapped out messages. One tap meant no, two taps maybe, and three taps yes.

When Madame Blavatsky investigated American mediums in 1875, she found that the Fox sisters had been left far behind. There was a woman in New York who could make spirits lift her piano and swing it from side to side while she played it. There was a woman in Boston who caused flowers and vines to fall from the ceiling as the dead appeared. And on and on.

Madame Blavatsky was amazed and frightened and skeptical. "I had never known or even seen a medium, nor ever found myself in a séance room, before March, 1873," she wrote. She was forty-two in 1873, and her head was buzzing with occult theories, but she was squeamish about contacts with the dead.

> It was in August of that year [she went on] that I learned for the first time in my life what was the philosophy of the Spiritualists. When I heard stated the claims of the American Spiritualists about the "Summer Land," etc., I rejected the whole thing point blank. I say again, I was never a Spiritualist.

But her mind was soon blown on a farm in Vermont. Listen to this: She investigated a 100-percent-American medium named William Eddy, in Chittenden Township, Vermont, and she was openly skeptical and sophisticated, and here is how William Eddy settled her hash: He summoned for Madame Blavatsky seven visible spirits which only she could have known about, and they spoke languages never heard in Vermont before or since.

He materialized a boy from the Russian state of Georgia, who chatted in colloquial Georgian and played on his guitar, at her request, the *lezginka,* a Circassian dance. He materialized Hassan Agha, a wealthy merchant from Tiflis, and Saffar Ali Bek, a Kurdish chieftain, who used to be Madame Blavatsky's companion on horseback trips in Armenia. He materialized a former Tartar servant of hers, who said, to her, *"Tchock yachtchi,"* which turns out to be the way the Tartars say, "All right."

He materialized an old Russian woman, who used to be H.P.B.'s sister's nurse, and an enormous black man in a fancy headdress, a magician H.P.B. had met in Africa.

Finally, he materialized an old man who wore around his neck the Russian decoration of St. Ann, which was suspended from the proper ribbon—red moiré with two black stripes. This last spook was her uncle.

This happened over a period of fourteen days. It was a splendid show, and I do not propose to reveal how the swindle was perpetrated.

And I have not yet described the grand finale. This was it: A spook named George Dix appeared and said this to Madame Blavatsky: "Madame, I am now about to give you a test of genuineness of the manifestations of this circle, which I think will satisfy not only you, but a skeptical world beside. I shall place in your hand the buckle of a medal of honor worn in life by your brave father and buried with his body in Russia."

This the spirit did.

Forty thousand Earthlings belong today to the Theosophical Society, which Madame Blavatsky and a Civil War veteran named Colonel Henry S. Olcott founded in 1875. (Over the years the society has attracted such distinguished people as Thomas A. Edison; General Abner Doubleday, the so-called inventor of baseball; the poet W. B. Yeats; the nineteenth-century English reformer Dr. Annie Besant; Motilal Nehru, the father of the Indian premier; and the Dutch painter Piet Mondrian.) Five thousand of these inquisitive souls live in the U.S.A. Their headquarters are in exotic Wheaton, Illinois. They keep

Madame Blavatsky's amazing writings in print. Like the late Fred Allen, H.P.B. may actually have written more than she could lift.

Here is a random sample of her writing, taken from *The Voice of Silence:*

> In order to become the KNOWER OF ALL-SELF thou hast first of SELF to be the knower. To reach the knowledge of that SELF thou hast to give up Self to Non-Self, Being to Non-Being, and then thou canst repose between the wings of the GREAT BIRD. Aye, sweet is rest between the wings of that which is not born, nor dies, but is the AUM throughout eternal ages.

Here is another sample, from *The Secret Doctrine* this time, a 1,300-page work H.P.B. wrote without once cracking a reference book.

> It is the Moon that plays the largest and most important part in the formation of the Earth itself, as in the peopling thereof with human beings. The Lunar Monads or Pitris, the ancestors of man, become in reality man himself. They are the Monads who enter on the cycle of evolution on Globe A, and who, passing around the Chain of planets, evolve the human form as has just been shown. At the beginning of the human stage of the Fourth Round on this Globe, they "ooze out" their astral doubles from the "ape-like" forms which they had evolved in Round Three.

And so on.

This was the sort of wisdom Madame Blavatsky felt she was destined to bring to America, stuff learned from masters in Tibet and India and Egypt and the African interior.

She arrived here feeling like a treasure ship laden with glittering mysteries. And then she herself was dumfounded (briefly) by the ghoulish games our own rustic magicians were into.

The Theosophical Society does not hold séances, has no rituals or places of worship. It praises worldwide brotherhood, suggests that there is much to be learned from all religions, and calmly reminds all who will listen that there are many odd and important adventures in life which science cannot explain. The society would welcome explanations.

It is beautifully candid about Madame Blavatsky. It gladly publishes her *Personal Memoirs,* though these often reveal a woman who was not only homely, but sometimes ridiculous and perhaps mentally ill. The *Memoirs* aren't actually memoirs, by the way. They are a posthumous pasticcio of letters and diary entries and so on, not only by Madame Blavatsky, but by her friends and relatives.

The society doesn't mind if we learn from the *Memoirs,* for instance, that Madame Blavatsky when a child "was often scared into fits through her own hallucinations." An aunt recalls this, and the aunt goes on:

> She felt certain of being persecuted by what she called "the terrible glaring eyes," invisible to everyone else. . . . At other times she would be seized with fits of laughter, explaining them as responses to the amusing tricks of her invisible companions.

So much for what these days we call mental illness.

As for ridiculousness: One morning in New York City, Madame Blavatsky couldn't come to breakfast until somebody rescued her. Spirits had sewed her nightgown to the mattress.

Another time a handsome spirit did his self-portrait in oils and ordered H.P.B. to decorate the frame with painted flowers, a chore she detested.

And so on.

She could cause her palms to exude sandalwood perfume whenever anybody wanted some.

But the woman had greatness, all the same. This would be a drab and empty world indeed if it weren't for zany women and men. She was so *brave,* to begin with, traveling so far alone. She was so brilliant, mastering a dozen or more languages, in order to learn what local wise men knew. And she was so generous, wanting almost nothing for herself—longing for a far more glamorous and complicated spiritual life for all mankind.

And she was scared to death that untrained, unworthy persons would tinker with magic and raise hell. She made enemies in America by saying that mediums were taking ghastly risks with forces they did not understand.

She sometimes wrote clearly and simply, as here:

> It is the motive, and the motive alone, which makes any exercise of power become *black, malignant,* or *white, beneficent Magic.* It is impossible to employ spiritual forces if there is the slightest tinge of selfishness remaining in the operator. For, unless the intention is entirely unalloyed, the spiritual will transform itself into the psychic, will act on the astral plane, and dire results may be produced by it. The powers and forces of animal nature can equally be used by the selfish and revengeful, as by the unselfish and the all-forgiving; the powers and forces of spirit lend

themselves only to the perfectly pure in heart—and this is DIVINE MAGIC.

(This quotation is from H.P.B.'s *Studies in Occultism,* by the way, and the strident use of capital letters is hers.)

So, like so many holy people, she tried hard to be pure. She wrote a list of rules for purity, which she had learned in India and Tibet. And, as might be expected, these prohibited bodily contact, the eating of meat, the use of wine and spirits and opium, demanded the renunciation of all the vanities of life and the world, and recommended much meditation.

When she had only one more year to live, enemies accused her in the New York *Sun* of having been a member of the demimonde at one time, of having borne an illegitimate son. She sued, and the story was retracted. She was prepared to offer in evidence the results of a gynecological examination, which stated that she could never have had children and could never have had connection with a man without its being painful.

She was a widow, it's true, having been married at sixteen to General N. V. Blavatsky, a man at least three times her age. But her aunt says that she fled from her husband right after the ceremony, "without giving him any opportunity to ever even *think* of her as his wife." And her travels around the world began.

Here is an undated note from a sketchbook she kept from about her sixteenth year onward: "Woman finds her happiness in the acquisition of supernatural powers. Love is but a vile dream, a nightmare."

Maybe so.

Kurt Vonnegut, Jr.

And *even* so, most of her friends were men. "Till nine years of age, in my father's regiment," she said, "the only nurses I knew were artillery soldiers and Buddhist Calmucks." Her mother was Hélène de Hahn, a novelist who was called by one critic the "Russian Georges Sand." (Her pen name was "Zenaida R." I have not read her.) This was an amazing sort of mother to have, but Madame Blavatsky in her *Memoirs* declines to be amazed. Here is all she says about her: "My Mother died when my brother was born, six months after, in 1840 or 1839—I can't be sure." Interestingly, she was wrong about her mother's death date, which was 1842. So, in her imagination, she made her mother's pitifully short life even shorter than it was.

So Madame Blavatsky was eleven years old when her mother died, and her younger sister recalls this scene:

> When our mother was dying . . . she was filled with well-founded apprehensions for her eldest daughter's future, and said: "Ah well! Perhaps it is best that I am dying, so at least I shall be spared seeing what befalls Helena! Of one thing I am certain, her life will not be as that of other women, and she will have much to suffer."

Can we safely conclude from this, 128 years later, that mother and daughter did not get along well? Perhaps.

One thing we can be sure about: Madame Blavatsky even in childhood hated all things most women are supposed to love, possibly because she was so husky. When she was sweet sixteen, for instance, she was living with her grandparents, and they felt she should go to a ball. They felt this strongly. They said they would use force if they had to. So, according to Madame Blavatsky's own account, she put her foot in boiling water. She was an invalid for six months after that.

Some virgin!

After her foot healed, she married old General Blavatsky and fled around the world three times, and she learned all sorts of magic tricks—from sleight of hand to hypnotism to ancient procedures that may have resulted in what we might call miracles.

Miracles.

She found the world so marvelous, it seems to me, because she was so ravenous for marvels and because she was able to persuade herself and others that marvels were what they had seen. Even as a motherless child in her grandparents' spooky house, she seems to have had the same sort of hypnotic magnetism that would allow Rasputin to dominate the Russian royal family seventy years later.

For instance: Her sister Vera remembered her as an astonishingly vivid storyteller as a child. "She used to dream aloud and tell us of her visions," she wrote, ". . . as palpable as life to her!" One time she stood on a patch of sand and told of the sea and the plants and monsters that had lived in it millions of years before. She suddenly brought the dream into the present. "We *are* surrounded with water! We are *amid* the mysteries of a submarine world!" she cried.

> She was speaking with such conviction [said her sister], and her voice had such a ring of real amazement and horror, and her childish face wore such a look of wild joy and terror at the same time, that when . . . she fell down on the sand, screaming at the

top of her voice . . . every one of us fell down on our faces, as desperately screaming and as fully convinced that the sea had engulfed us, and that we were no more.

She visited relatives in Russia years later, after she had learned some new tricks. Her brother was skeptical of her Marco Polo yarns; dared her to show him something he couldn't explain. So she told him to lift a small chess table, which was easy to do. Then she stared at the table, but didn't touch it, and she defied him to lift it again. He might as well have tried to hoist the Kremlin. Other heroes had a go at the hoodooed table, too, and they split it—but it wouldn't leave the floor.

Madame Blavatsky pronounced the table light as a feather once more, and lo, it was so.

I call this hypnotism.

My calling it that is talking through my hat, of course. That was a long time ago, and I haven't found any admissions by Madame Blavatsky that she was a hypnotist. And I talk through my hat again when I say that she was enchantingly clever at mechanical parlor tricks, sleight of hand, and so on—with a little ventriloquism thrown in from time to time.

I will dream on about her, having read a lot about her, and conclude that she was not only profoundly religious but, on occasion, playful to the point of rascality. Consider the way she bamboozled a New York visitor named Mr. W. Q. Judge with a little Chinese cabinet on her writing table. It had many small drawers. "It was an ordinary cabinet of its class," Mr. Judge later wrote. Ha!

Many a time has one of those drawers become the vanishing point of various articles, and as often, on the other hand, was the birthplace of some object which had not before been seen in the rooms. I have often seen her put small coins or a ring or an amulet in a drawer, close it, almost instantly, reopen it, and nothing was visible.

Ha!

The cofounder of the Theosophical Society, along with Madame Blavatsky, as I've already said, was Colonel Henry S. Olcott, a divorced lawyer when they met. One day he brought her some material for towels. It had to be cut up and hemmed. While Madame Blavatsky was doing the hemming, Colonel Olcott saw her kicking and joking with something invisible under the table. He asked her what the invisible thing was, and she replied, "Oh, it is only a little beast of an elemental that pulled my dress and wants something to do."

So Colonel Olcott told her to have the elemental hem the towels, since she was a miserable seamstress and a rotten sport about household chores in general.

So she put the unhemmed towels into a bookcase with glass doors and locked the doors. And she and the colonel chatted about occult matters for about twenty minutes, until a sort of mouse squeak came from under the worktable. The colonel unlocked the bookcase. Guess what he found.

The towels were all badly hemmed.

Colonel Olcott, by the way, had not led the life of a chowderhead. He was a distinguished officer in the Civil War and a slashing crusader against Army graft. He was also an agricultural innovator, experimenting successfully with new strains of sugarcane that were hardy in temperate climates. He reminds me of Henry A. Wallace somewhat. Wallace, Franklin D. Roosevelt's Secretary of Agriculture for a while, also experimented with new plant strains and became enthusiastic about occultism toward the end of his life.

Colonel Olcott was for a while so respected for his soundness of mind that he was made a member of an elite committee of three, whose purpose was to discover the extent of the conspiracy that led to the death of Abraham Lincoln.

Finally, he was a distinguished attorney, whose work in the area of insurance law continues to be influential today.

Be that as it may, he believed with all his heart that a good fairy of some kind hemmed those towels.

And he was well into believing seemingly impossible things before Madame Blavatsky came along. They met at the Eddy home in Vermont, where she received her dead father's buckle for a souvenir.

> My eye was first attracted by a scarlet Garibaldian shirt Madame Blavatsky wore [Colonel Olcott later wrote], as in vivid contrast with the dull colors around. Her hair was then a thick blonde mop, worn shorter than the shoulders, and it stood out from her head, silken-soft and crinkled to the roots, like the fleece of a Cotswold ewe. . . . Madame Blavatsky rolled herself a cigarette, for which I offered her a light as a pretext to enter into conversation.

Kismet.

They adored each other at once, with a purity unsoiled by sex. The colonel was a divorced man, wandering farther and farther from the law profession and deeper and

134

deeper into spiritualism—and she was a widow who liked to be called Jack. Both were forty-three.

They had many absorbing adventures, at first investigating American mediums, most of whom they denounced as fakes. Their favorite technique for terrifying a fake was to attend a séance run by the fake—and materialize a *real* spirit.

They never lived together, but they were seldom apart for long, and here is an American idyll from Victorian or Ulysses S. Grantian times: Colonel Olcott often kept Madame Blavatsky company while she wrote at night. And he tells us that she chain-smoked as she wrote, and rolled cigarettes with one hand. Meanwhile, large balls of light crept over the furniture or jumped from point to point, "while the most beautiful liquid bell-sounds now and again burst out from the air of the room."

I find that I believe this.

> I was sent to America on purpose [Madame Blavatsky wrote]. There I found Olcott in love with spirits, as he became in love with the Masters later on. I was ordered to let him know that spiritual phenomena without the philosophy of occultism were dangerous and misleading. I proved to him that all that mediums could do through spirits, others could do at will without any spirits at all; that bells and thought-reading, raps and physical phenomena, could be achieved by anyone who had a faculty of acting in his physical body through the organs of his astral body; and I had the faculty ever since I was four years old.

They founded the sane and altruistic Theosophical Society in 1875. Blavatsky and Olcott later traveled to the

Far East, where the colonel learned to work a few small miracles of his own. Madame Blavatsky never returned to America, or to Russia, either. She spent the last five years of her life with friends in Europe and England, writing a lot, not creating much of a public stir.

She died in London in 1891. She was the first Russian woman ever to have become an American citizen.

I have at hand a letter from Joy Mills, national president of the Theosophical Society in America, and she says to me:

> It is often regrettable that erroneous statements concerning Madame Blavatsky have been perpetuated in
> - print so that present-day researchers may at times unknowingly continue allegations and accusations that are not only malicious but quite false. We are therefore eager to assist anyone seeking to learn the truth concerning the life and teachings of this remarkable woman of the last century.

All I can say in reply is that I have approached Madame Blavatsky from inside, so to speak, have listened to her and those who loved her. I might as easily have assumed that her life was a low comedy, might have eagerly quoted her many enemies, who thought she was a graceless fraud.

At a minimum: Madame Blavatsky brought America wisdom from the East, which it very much needed, which it still very much needs. If she garbled or invented some of that wisdom, she was doing no worse than other teachers have done. The only greed I can detect in the woman is a greed to be *believed*.

So I say, "Peace and honor to Madame Blavatsky." I

am charmed and amused that she was an American citizen for a little while. That was a bureaucratic detail, of course. Bizarre as she may have been, she was something quite lovely: She thought all human beings were her brothers and sisters—she was a citizen of the world. She said this among other things:

> *Let not the fierce sun dry one tear of pain*
> *Before thyself hast wiped it from the sufferer's eye.*

Cheers.

Biafra:
A People
Betrayed

THERE is a "Kingdom of Biafra" on some old maps which were made by early white explorers of the west coast of Africa. Nobody is now sure what that kingdom was—what its laws and arts and tools were like. No tales survive of the kings and queens.

As for the "Republic of Biafra": We know a great deal. It was a nation with more citizens than Ireland and Norway combined. It proclaimed itself an independent republic on May 30, 1967. On January 17 of 1970, it surrendered unconditionally to Nigeria, the nation from which it had tried to secede. It had few friends in this world, and among its active enemies were Russia and Great Britain. Its enemies were pleased to call it a "tribe."

Some tribe.

The Biafrans were mainly Christians—and they spoke

English melodiously, and their economy was this one: small-town free enterprise. The worthless Biafran currency was gravely honored to the end.

The tune of Biafra's national anthem was *Finlandia,* by Jan Sibelius. The equatorial Biafrans admired the arctic Finns because the Finns won and kept their freedom in spite of ghastly odds.

Biafra lost its freedom, of course, and I was in the middle of it as all its fronts were collapsing. I flew in from Gabon on the night of January 3, with bags of corn, beans, and powdered milk—aboard a blacked-out DC-6 chartered by Caritas, the Roman Catholic relief organization. I flew out six nights later on an empty DC-4 chartered by the French Red Cross. It was the last plane to leave Biafra that was not fired upon.

While in Biafra, I saw a play which expressed the spiritual condition of the Biafrans at the end. It was set in ancient times, in the home of a medicine man. The moon had not been seen for many months, and the crops had failed. There was nothing to eat anymore. A sacrifice was made to a goddess of fertility, and the sacrifice was refused. The goddess gave the reason: The people were not sufficiently unselfish and brave.

Before the drama began, the national anthem was played on an ancient marimba. It seems likely that similar marimbas were heard in the court of the Kingdom of Biafra. The black man who played the marimba was naked to the waist. He squatted on the stage. He was a composer. He also held a doctor's degree from the London School of Economics.

Some tribe.

Biafra: A People Betrayed

I went to Biafra with another novelist, my old friend Vance Bourjaily, and with Miss Miriam Reik, who would be our guide. She was head of a pro-Biafran committee that had already flown several American writers into Biafra. She would pay our way.

I met her for the first time at Kennedy Airport. We were about to take off for Paris together. It was New Year's Day. I bought her a drink, though she protested that her committee should pay, and I learned that she had a doctor's degree in English literature. She was also a pianist and a daughter of Theodor Reik, the famous psychoanalyst.

Her father had died three days before.

I told Miriam how sorry I was about her father, said how much I'd liked the one book of his I had read, which was *Listening with the Third Ear.*

He was a gentle Jew, who got out of Austria while the getting was good. Another well-known book of his was *Masochism in Modern Man.*

And I asked her to tell me more about her committee, whose beneficiary I was, and she confessed that she was it: It was a committee of one. She is a tall, good-looking woman, by the way, thirty-two years old. She said she founded her own committee because she grew sick of other American organizations that were helping Biafra. Those organizations teemed with people who were kinky with guilt, she said. They were trying to dump some of that guilt by being maudlinly charitable. As for herself, she said, it was the greatness of the Biafran people, not their pitifulness, that turned her on.

She hoped the Biafrans would get more weapons from somebody—the very latest in killing machines.

She was going into Biafra for the third time in a year. She wasn't afraid of anything. Some committee.

I admire Miriam, though I am not grateful for the trip she gave me. It was like a free trip to Auschwitz when the ovens were still going full blast. I now feel lousy all the time.

I will follow Miriam's example as best I can. My main aim will not be to move readers to voluptuous tears with tales about innocent black children dying like flies, about rape and looting and murder and all that. I will tell instead about an admirable nation that lived for less than three years.

De mortuis nil nisi bonum. Say nothing but good of the dead.

I asked a Biafran how long his nation had existed so far, and he replied, "Three Christmases—and a little bit more." He wasn't a hungry baby. He was a hungry man. He was a living skeleton, but he walked like a man.

Miriam Reik and I picked up Vance Bourjaily in Paris, and we flew down to Gabon and then into Biafra. The only way to get into Biafra was at night by air. There were only eight passenger seats at the rear of the cabin. The rest of the cabin was heaped with bags of food. The food was from America.

We flew over water; there were Russian trawlers below. They were monitoring every plane that came into Biafra. The Russians were helpful in a lot of ways: They gave the Nigerians Ilyushin bombers and MIGs and heavy artillery. And the British gave the Nigerians artillery, too— and advisers, and tanks and armored cars, and machine guns and mortars and all that, and endless ammunition.

America was neutral.

When we got close to the one remaining Biafran airport,

which was a stretch of highway, its lights came on. It was a secret. Its lights resembled two rows of glowworms.

The moment our wheels touched the runway, the runway lights went out and our plane's headlights came on. Our plane slowed down, pulled off the runway, killed its lights, and then everything was pitch black again.

There were only two white faces in the crowd around our plane. One was a Holy Ghost Father. The other was a doctor from the French Red Cross. The doctor ran a hospital for the children who were suffering from kwashiorkor, the pitiful children who had no protein.

Father.

Doctor.

As I write, Nigeria has arrested all the Holy Ghost Fathers, who stayed to the end with their people in Biafra. The priests were mostly Irishmen. They were beloved. Whenever they built a church, they also built a school.

Children and simple men and women thought all white men were priests, so they would often beam at Vance or me and say, "Hello, Father."

The Fathers are now being deported forever. Their crime: compassion in time of war.

We were taken to the Frenchman's hospital the next morning, in a chauffeur-driven Peugeot. The name of the village itself sounded like the wail of a child: Awo-Omama.

I said to an educated Biafran, "Americans may not know much about Biafra, but they know about the children."

"We're grateful," he replied, "but I wish they knew more than that. They think we're a dying nation. We aren't. We're an energetic, modern nation that is being born! We have doctors. We have hospitals. We have public-health programs. If we have so much sickness, it is because our enemies have designed every diplomatic and military move with one end in mind—that we starve to death."

About kwashiorkor: It is a rare disease, caused by a lack of protein. Its cure has been easy—until the blockading of Biafra.

The worst sufferers there were the children of refugees, driven from their homes, then driven off the roads and into the bush by MIGs and armored columns. The Biafrans weren't jungle people. They were village people—farmers and professionals and clerks and businessmen. They had no weapons to hunt with. Back in the bush, they fed their children whatever roots and fruit they were lucky enough to find. At the end, a very common diet was water and thin air.

So the children came down with kwashiorkor, no longer a rare disease.

The child's hair turned red. His skin split like the skin of a ripe tomato. His rectum protruded. His arms and legs were like lollipop sticks.

Vance and Miriam and I waded through shoals of children like those at Awo-Omama. We discovered that if we let our hands dangle down among the children, a child would grasp each finger or thumb—five children to a hand. A finger from a stranger, miraculously, would allow a child to stop crying for a while.

A MIG came over, fired a few rounds, didn't hit anything this time, though the hospital had been hit often before. Our guide guessed that the pilot was an Egyptian or an East German.

I asked a Biafran nurse what sort of supplies the hospital was most in need of.

Her answer: "Food."

Biafra had a George Washington—for three Christmases and a little bit more. He was and is Odumegwu Ojukwu. Like George Washington, General Ojukwu was one of the most prosperous men of his place and time. He was a graduate of Sandhurst, Britain's West Point.

The three of us spent an hour with him. He shook our hands at the end. He thanked us for coming. "If we go forward, we die," he said. "If we go backward, we die. So we go forward." He was ten years younger than Vance and me. I found him perfectly enchanting. Many people mock him now. They think he should have died with his troops.

Maybe so.

If he had died, he would have been one more corpse in millions.

He was a calm, heavy man when we met him. He chain-smoked. Cigarettes were worth a blue million in Biafra. He wore a camouflage jacket, though he was sitting in a cool living room in a velveteen easy chair. "I should warn you," he said, "we are in range of their artillery."

His humor was gallows humor, since everything was falling apart around his charisma and air of quiet confidence. His humor was superb.

Later, when we met his second-in-command, General Philip Effiong, he, too, turned out to be a gallows humorist. Vance said this: "Effiong *should* be the number-two man. He's the second funniest man in Biafra."

Jokes.

Miriam was annoyed by my conversation at one point,

and she said scornfully, "You won't open your mouth unless you can make a joke." It was true. Joking was my response to misery I couldn't do anything about.

The jokes of Ojukwu and Effiong had to do with the crime for which the Biafrans were being punished so hideously by so many nations. The crime: They were attempting to become a nation themselves.

"They call us a dot on the map," said General Ojukwu, "and nobody's sure quite where."

Inside that dot were 700 lawyers, 500 physicians, 300 engineers, 8 million poets, 2 novelists of the first rank, and God only knows what else—about one-third of all the black intellectuals in Africa. Some dot.

Those intellectuals had once fanned out all over Nigeria, where they had been envied and lynched and massacred. So they retreated to their homeland, to the dot.

The dot has now vanished. Hey, presto.

When we met General Ojukwu, his soldiers were going into battle with thirty-five rounds of rifle ammunition. There was no more where that came from. For weeks before that, they had been living on one cup of gari a day. The recipe for gari is this: Add water to pulverized cassava root.

Now the soldiers didn't even have gari anymore.

General Ojukwu described a typical Nigerian attack for us: "They pound a position with artillery for twenty-four hours, then they send forward one armored car. If anybody shoots at it, it retreats, and another twenty-four hours of bombardment begins. When the infantry moves forward, they drive a screen of refugees before them."

We asked him what was becoming of the refugees now

in Nigerian hands. He had no jokes on this subject. He said leadenly that the men, women, and children were formed into three groups, which were led away separately. "Your guess is as good as mine," he said, "as to what happens after that," and he paused. Then he finished the sentence: "To the men and the women and the children."

We were given private rooms and baths in what had been a teachers' college in Owerri, the capital of Biafra. The town had been captured by the Nigerians, and then, in the one great Biafran victory of the war, recaptured by the Biafrans.

We were taken to a training camp near Owerri. The soldiers had no live ammunition. In mock attacks, the riflemen shouted, *"Bang!"* The machine gunners shouted, *"Bup-bup-bup!"*

And the officer who showed us around, also a graduate of Sandhurst, said, "There wouldn't be all this fuss, you know, if it weren't for the petroleum." He was speaking of the vast oil field beneath our feet.

We asked him who owned the oil, and I expected him to say ringingly that it was the property of the Biafran people now. But he didn't. "We never nationalized it," he said. "It still belongs to British Petroleum and Shell."

He wasn't bitter. I never met a bitter Biafran.

General Ojukwu gave us a clue, I think, as to why the Biafrans were able to endure so much so long without bitterness: They all had the emotional and spiritual strength that an enormous family can give. We asked the general to tell us about his family, and he answered that it was three thousand members strong. He knew every member of it by face, by name, and by reputation.

A more typical Biafran family might consist of a few hundred souls. And there were no orphanages, no old people's homes, no public charities—and, early in the war, there weren't even schemes for taking care of refugees. The families took care of their own—perfectly naturally.

The families were rooted in land. There was no Biafran so poor that he did not own a garden.

Lovely.

Families met often, men and women alike, to vote on family matters. When war came, there was no conscription. The families decided who should go.

In happier times, the families voted on who should go to college—to study what and where. Then everybody chipped in for clothes and transportation and tuition. The first person from the area to be sponsored by his family all the way through graduate school was a physician, who received his doctor's degree in 1938. Thus began a mania for higher education of all kinds.

This mania probably did more to doom the Biafrans than any quantity of petroleum. When Nigeria became a nation in 1960, formed from two British colonies, Biafra was part of it—and Biafrans got the best jobs in industry and the civil service and the hospitals and the schools, because they were so well educated.

They were hated for that—perfectly naturally.

It was peaceful in Owerri at first. It took us a few days to catch on: Not only Owerri but all of Biafra was about to fall. Even as we arrived, government offices nearby were preparing to move. I learned something: Capitals can fall almost silently.

Nobody warned us. Everybody we talked to smiled. And the smile we saw most frequently belonged to Dr. B. N. Unachukwu, the chief of protocol in the Ministry of Affairs. Think of that: Biafra was so poor in allies at the end that the chief of protocol had nothing better to do than woo two novelists and an English teacher.

He made lists of appointments we had with ministers and writers and educators and so on. He sent around a car each morning, with a chauffeur and guide. And then we caught on: His smile and everybody's smile was becoming slightly sicker with each passing day.

On our fifth day in Biafra, there was no Dr. Unachukwu, no chauffeur, and no guide.

We waited and waited on our porches. Chinua Achebe, the young novelist, came by. We asked him if he had any news. He said he didn't listen to news anymore. He didn't smile. He seemed to be listening to something melancholy and maybe beautiful, far far away.

I had a novel of his, *Things Fall Apart.* He autographed it for me. "I would invite you to my house," he said, "but we don't have *anything.* "

A truck went by, loaded with office furniture. All the trucks had names painted on their sides. The name of that one was *Slow to Anger.*

"There must be *some* news," I insisted.

"News?" he echoed. He thought. Then he said dreamily, "They have just found a mass grave outside the prison wall." There had been a rumor, he explained, that the Nigerians had shot a lot of civilians while they'd held Owerri. Now the graves had been found.

"Graves," said Chinua Achebe. He found them uninteresting.

"What are you writing now?" said Miriam.

"Writing?" he said. It was obvious that he wasn't writing anything, that he was simply waiting for the end. "A dirge in Ibo," he said. Ibo was his native tongue.

149

An extraordinarily pretty girl named Rosemary Egonsu Ezirim came over to introduce herself. She was a zoologist. She had been working on a project that hoped to turn the streams into fish hatcheries. "The project has been suspended temporarily," she said, "so I am writing poems."

"All projects have been suspended temporarily," said Chinua, "so we are *all* writing poems."

Leonard Hall, of the Manchester *Guardian,* stopped by. He said, "You know, the closest parallel to what Biafra is going through was the Jews in the Warsaw ghetto." He was right. The Jews of Warsaw understood that they were going to get killed, no matter what they did, so they died fighting.

The Biafrans kept telling the outside world that Nigeria wanted to kill them all, but the outside world was unimpressed.

"It's hard to prove genocide," said Hall. "If some Biafrans survive, then genocide hasn't been committed. If no Biafrans survive, who will complain?"

A male refugee came up to us, rubbed his belly with one hand, begged with the other. He rolled his eyes.

"No chop," we said. That meant, "No food." That was what one said to beggars.

Then a healthy girl offered us a quart of honey for three pounds. As I've already said, the economy was free enterprise to the end.

It was a lazy day.

We asked Rosemary about a round, bright-orange button she was wearing. "Daughters of Biafra," it said. "Wake! March!" In the middle was a picture of a rifle.

Rosemary explained that the Daughters of Biafra supported the troops in various ways, comforted the wounded, and practiced guerrilla warfare. "We go up into the front lines when we can," she said. "We bring the men small presents. If they haven't been doing well, we scold them, and they promise to do better. We tell them that they will know when things are really bad, because the women will come into the trenches to fight. Women are much stronger and braver than men."

Maybe so.

"Chinua, what can we send you when we get back home?" said Vance.

And Chinua said, "Books."

"Rosemary," I said, "where do you live?"

"In a dormitory room not far from here. Would you like to see it?" she said.

So Vance and I walked over there with her, to stretch our legs. On the way, we marveled at a squash court built of cement block—built, no doubt, in colonial times. It had been turned into a Swiss cheese by armor-piercing cannon shells. There was a naked child in the doorway, and her hair was red. She seemed very sleepy, and the light hurt her eyes.

"Hello, Father," she said.

All of Owerri seemed out for a walk—on either side of the street in single file. The files moved in opposite directions and circulated about the town. There was no place in particular for most of us to go. We were simply the restless center of the dot on the map called Biafra, and the dot was growing smaller all the time.

We strolled past a row of neat bungalows. Civil servants lived there. Each house had a car out front—a VW, an Opel, a Peugeot. These were privately owned. There was plenty of gasoline, because the Biafrans had built cunning

151

refineries in the bush. There weren't many storage batteries, though. Most private cars had to be started by pushing.

Outside one bungalow was an Opel station wagon with its back full of parcels and with a bed and a baby carriage tied on top. The man of the house was testing the knots he'd tied, while his wife stood by with the baby in her arms. They were going on a family trip to nowhere.

We gave them a push.

A soldier awarded Vance and me a salute and a dazzling smile. *"Comment ça va?"* he said. He supposed we were Frenchmen. He liked us for that. France had slipped a few weapons to Biafra. So had Rhodesia and South Africa— and so had Israel, I suspect.

"We will accept help from anyone," General Ojukwu told us, "no matter what their reasons are for giving it. Wouldn't you?"

Rosemary lived in a twelve-by-twelve dormitory room with her five younger brothers and sisters, who had come to see her over the Christmas holidays. Rosemary and her seventeen-year-old sister had the bed. The rest slept on mats on the floor, and everybody was having an awfully good time.

There was plenty to eat. There were about twenty pounds of yams piled on the windowsill. There was a quart of palm oil for frying yams.

Palm oil, incidentally, was one of two commodities that had induced white men to colonize the area so long ago. The other commodity was even more valuable than palm oil. It was human slaves.

Think of that: slaves.

We asked Rosemary's sister how long it took her to fix her hair and whether she could do it without assistance.

She had about fourteen pigtails sticking straight out from her head. Not only that, but her scalp was crisscrossed by bare strips, which formed diamonds—strips around the hair in the pigtails. Her head was splendidly complicated, like a Russian Easter egg.

"Oh, no—I could never do it alone," she said. Her relatives did it for her every morning. It took them an hour, she said.

Relatives.

She was an innocent, pretty dumpling in a metropolis for the first time. Her village hadn't been overrun yet. Her big, cozy family hadn't been scattered to the winds. There were peace and plenty there.

"I think we must be the luckiest people in Biafra," she said.

Rosemary's sister still had her baby fat.

And now, as I write, I hear from my radio that there was a lot of raping when the Nigerian army came through, that one woman who resisted was drenched with gasoline and then set on fire.

I have cried only once about Biafra. I did it three days after I got home—at two o'clock in the morning. I made grotesque little barking sounds for about a minute and a half, and that was that.

Miriam tells me that she hasn't cried yet. She's tough about the ways of the world.

Vance cried at least once—while we were still in Biafra. When little children took hold of his fingers and stopped crying, Vance burst into tears.

Wounded soldiers were living in Rosemary's dormitory, too. As I left her room, I tripped on her doorsill, and a wounded soldier in the corridor said brightly, "Sorry, sah!" This was a form of politeness I had never encountered outside Biafra. Whenever I did something clumsy or unlucky, a Biafran was sure to say that: "Sorry, sah!" He would be genuinely sorry. He was on *my* side, and against a booby-trapped universe.

Vance came into the corridor, dropped the lens cap of his camera. "Sorry, sah!" said the soldier again.

We asked him if life had been terrible at the front.

"Yes, sah!" he said. "But you remind yourself that you are a brave Biafran soldier, sah, and you stay."

A dinner party was given in our honor that night by Dr. Ifegwu Eke, the commissioner for education, and his wife. They had been married four days. He had a doctor's degree from Harvard. She had a doctor's degree from Columbia. There were five other guests. They all had doctor's degrees.

We were inside a bungalow. The draperies were drawn. There was a Danish modern sideboard on which primitive African carvings were displayed. There was a stereophonic phonograph as big as a boxcar. It was playing the music of Mantovani. One of the syrupy melodies, I remember, was "Born Free."

There were canapés. There was a sip of brandy to loosen our tongues. There was a buffet dinner, which included bits of meat from a small native antelope. It was dreadful in the way so many parties are dreadful: Everybody talked about everything except what was really on his mind.

The guest to my right was Dr. S. J. S. Cookey, who had taken his degree at Oxford and who was now provincial administrator for Opobo Province. He was exhausted. His eyes were red. Opobo Province had fallen to the Nigerians months ago.

Others were chatting prettily, so I ransacked my mind for items that might encourage Dr. Cookey and me to bubble, too. But all I could think of were gruesome realities of the most immediate sort. It occurred to me to ask him, for instance, if there was a chance that one thing that had killed so many Biafrans was the arrogance of Biafra's intellectuals. My mind was eager to ask him, too, if I had been a fool to be charmed by General Ojukwu. Was he yet another great leader who would never surrender, who became holier and more radiant as his people died for him?

So I turned to cement. I remained cement through the rest of the evening, and so did Dr. Cookey.

Vance and Miriam and I had a drink in Miriam's room after the party. Owerri's diesel generator had gone off for the night, so we lit a candle.

Miriam commented on my behavior at the party.

"I'm sorry," I said. "I didn't come to Biafra for canapés."

What did we eat in Biafra? As guests of the government, we had meat and yams and soups and fruit. It was embarrassing. Whenever we told a cadaverous beggar "No chop," it wasn't really true. We had plenty of chop, but it was all in our bellies.

There was a knock on Miriam's door that night. Three men came in. We were astonished. One of them was General Philip Effiong, the second funniest man in Biafra. He had a tremblingly devoted aide with him, who saluted him ten times a minute, though the general begged him not to. The third man was a suave and dapper civilian in white pants and sandals and a crimson dashiki. He was Mike Ikenze, personal press secretary to General Ojukwu.

The young general was boisterous, wry, swashbuckling —high as a kite on incredibly awful news from the fronts. Why did he come to see us? Here is my guess: He couldn't tell his own people how bad things were, and he had to tell somebody. We were the only foreigners around.

He talked for three hours. The Nigerians had broken through everywhere. They were fanning out fast, slicing the Biafran dot into dozens of littler ones. Inside some of these littler dots, hiding in the bush, were tens of thousands of Biafrans who had not eaten anything for two weeks and more.

What had become of the brave Biafran soldiers? They were woozy with hunger. They were palsied by shell shock. They had left their holes. They were wandering.

General Effiong threw up his hands. "It's over!" he cried, and he gave a laugh that was ghoulish and heartbroken. "If Biafra is now to become a tiny footnote in the history of mankind, let that footnote say, 'They attempted to give the world the first modern government in Africa. They failed.'

"The rest of the world thinks Nigeria can do no wrong," the general said. "I will make you a promise: Nigeria is going to disappoint the world so bitterly that it will take one generation for the world to get over the shock."

He was wrong, of course. The world is about as unshockable as a self-sealing gas tank.

We didn't hear guns until the next afternoon. At five o'clock sharp there were four quick peals of thunder to the south. The thunder was manmade. No shells came our way.

The birds stopped talking. Five minutes went by, and then they began talking again.

The government offices were all empty. So were the bungalows. We were waiting for Dr. Unachukwu to take us to Uli Airport, the only way out. The common people had stayed to the last, buying and selling and begging—doing each other's hair.

They, too, stopped talking when they heard the guns. We could see many of them from our porches. They did not start talking again. They gathered together their property, which they put on their heads. They walked out of Owerri wordlessly, away from the guns.

Dr. Unachukwu, our official host, did not come, and did not come. It was spooky in Owerri. We were now the only people there. We didn't hear the guns again. Their words to the wise were sufficient.

Owerri's diesel generator was still running. That was another thing I learned about a city falling silently: To fool the enemy for a little while, you leave the lights on.

Dr. Unachukwu came. He was frantic to be on his way, but he smiled and smiled. He was at the wheel of his own Mercedes. The back of it was crammed with boxes and suitcases. On top of the freight lay his eight-year-old son.

I have written all this quickly. I find that I have betrayed my promise to speak of the greatness rather than the pitifulness of the Biafran people. I have mourned the children copiously. I have told of a woman who was drenched in gasoline.

As for national greatness: It is probably true that all nations are great and even holy at the time of death.

The Biafrans had never fought before. They fought well this time. They will never fight again.

They will never play *Finlandia* on an ancient marimba again.

Peace.

My neighbors ask me what they can do for Biafra at this late date, or what they should have done for Biafra at some earlier date.

I tell them this: "Nothing. It was and is an internal Nigerian matter, which you can merely deplore."

Some wonder whether they, in order to be up-to-date, should hate Nigerians now.

I tell them, "No."

Address to Graduating Class at Bennington College, 1970

I HOPE you will be very happy as members of the educated class in America. I myself have been rejected again and again.

As I said on Earth Day in New York City not long ago: It isn't often that a total pessimist is invited to speak in the springtime. I predicted that everything would become worse, and everything has become worse.

One trouble, it seems to me, is that the majority of the

159

people who rule us, who have our money and power, are lawyers or military men. The lawyers want to talk our problems out of existence. The military men want us to find the bad guys and put bullets through their brains. These are not always the best solutions—particularly in the fields of sewage disposal and birth control.

I demand that the administration of Bennington College establish an R.O.T.C. unit here. It is imperative that we learn more about military men, since they have so much of our money and power now. It is a great mistake to drive military men from college campuses and into ghettos like Fort Benning and Fort Bragg. Make them do what they do so proudly in the midst of men and women who are educated.

When I was at Cornell University, the experiences that most stimulated my thinking were in R.O.T.C.—the manual of arms and close-order drill, and the way the officers spoke to me. Because of the military training I received at Cornell, I became a corporal at the end of World War Two. After the war, as you know, I made a fortune as a pacifist.

You should not only have military men here, but their weapons, too—especially crowd-control weapons such as machine guns and tanks. There is a tendency among young people these days to form crowds. Young people owe it to themselves to understand how easily machine guns and tanks can control crowds.

There is a basic rule about tanks, and you should know it: The only man who ever beat a tank was John Wayne. And he was in another tank.

Now then—about machine guns: They work sort of like a garden hose, except they spray death. They should be approached with caution.

Address to Graduating Class at Bennington College, 1970

There is a lesson for all of us in machine guns and tanks: Work within the system.

How pessimistic am I, really? I was a teacher at the University of Iowa three years ago. I had hundreds of students. As nearly as I am able to determine, not one of my ex-students has seen fit to reproduce. The only other demonstration of such a widespread disinclination to reproduce took place in Tasmania in about 1800. Native Tasmanians gave up on babies and the love thing and all that when white colonists, who were criminals from England, hunted them for sport.

I used to be an optimist. This was during my boyhood in Indianapolis. Those of you who have seen Indianapolis will understand that it was no easy thing to be an optimist there. It was the 500-mile Speedway Race, and then 364 days of miniature golf, and then the 500-mile Speedway Race again.

My brother Bernard, who was nine years older, was on his way to becoming an important scientist. He would later discover that silver iodide particles could precipitate certain kinds of clouds as snow or rain. He made me very enthusiastic about science for a while. I thought scientists were going to find out exactly how everything worked, and then make it work better. I fully expected that by the time I was twenty-one, some scientist, maybe my brother, would have taken a color photograph of God Almighty— and sold it to *Popular Mechanics* magazine.

Scientific truth was going to make us *so* happy and comfortable.

What actually happened when I was twenty-one was that we dropped scientific truth on Hiroshima. We killed everybody there. And I had just come home from being a prisoner of war in Dresden, which I'd seen burned to the ground. And the world was just then learning how ghastly the German extermination camps had been. So I had a heart-to-heart talk with myself.

"Hey, Corporal Vonnegut," I said to myself, "maybe you were wrong to be an optimist. Maybe pessimism is the thing."

I have been a consistent pessimist ever since, with a few exceptions. In order to persuade my wife to marry me, of course, I had to promise her that the future would be heavenly. And then I had to lie about the future again every time I thought she should have a baby. And then I had to lie to her again every time she threatened to leave me because I was too pessimistic.

I saved our marriage many times by exclaiming, "Wait! Wait! I see light at the end of the tunnel at last!" And I wish I could bring light to *your* tunnels today. My wife begged me to bring you light, but there *is* no light. Everything is going to become unimaginably worse, and never get better again. If I lied to you about that, you would sense that I'd lied to you, and that would be another cause for gloom. We have enough causes for gloom.

I should like to give a motto to your class, a motto to your entire generation. It comes from my favorite Shakespearean play, which is *King Henry VI, Part Three*. In the first scene of Act Two, you will remember, Edward, Earl of March, who will later become King Edward IV, enters with Richard, who will later become Duke of Gloucester. They are the Duke of York's sons. They arrive at the head of their troops on a plain near Mortimer's Cross in Herefordshire and immediately receive news that their father has had his head cut off. Richard says this, among other things, and this is the motto I give you: "To weep is to make less the depth of grief."

Address to Graduating Class at Bennington College, 1970

Again: "To weep is to make less the depth of grief."

It is from this same play, which has been such a comfort to me, that we find the line, "The smallest worm will turn being trodden on." I don't have to tell you that the line is spoken by Lord Clifford in Scene One of Act Two. This is meant to be optimistic, I think, but I have to tell you that a worm can be stepped on in such a way that it can't possibly turn after you remove your foot.

I have performed this experiment for my children countless times. They are grown-ups now. They can step on worms now with no help from their Daddy. But let us pretend for a moment that worms can turn, *do* turn. And let us ask ourselves, "What would be a good, new direction for the worm of civilization to take?"

Well—it should go upward, if possible. Up is certainly better than down, or is widely believed to be. And we would be a lot safer if the Government would take its money out of science and put it into astrology and the reading of palms. I used to think that science would save us, and science certainly tried. But we can't stand any more tremendous explosions, either for or against democracy. Only in superstition is there hope. If you want to become a friend of civilization, then become an enemy of truth and a fanatic for harmless balderdash.

I know that millions of dollars have been spent to produce this splendid graduating class, and that the main hope of your teachers was, once they got through with you, that you would no longer be superstitious. I'm sorry —I have to undo that now. I beg you to believe in the most ridiculous superstition of all: that humanity is at the center of the universe, the fulfiller or the frustrator of the grandest dreams of God Almighty.

If you can believe that, and make others believe it, then

there might be hope for us. Human beings might stop treating each other like garbage, might begin to treasure and protect each other instead. Then it might be all right to have babies again.

Many of you will have babies anyway, if you're anything like me. To quote the poet Schiller: "Against stupidity the very gods themselves contend in vain."

About astrology and palmistry: They are good because they make people feel vivid and full of possibilities. They are communism at its best. Everybody has a birthday and almost everybody has a palm.

Take a seemingly drab person born on August 3, for instance. He's a Leo. He is proud, generous, trusting, energetic, domineering, and authoritative! All Leos are! He is ruled by the Sun! His gems are the ruby and the diamond! His color is orange! His metal is gold! This is a *nobody*?

His harmonious signs for business, marriage, or companionship are Sagittarius and Aries. Anybody here a Sagittarius or an Aries? Watch out! Here comes destiny!

Is this lonely-looking human being really alone? Far from it! He shares the sign of Leo with T. E. Lawrence, Herbert Hoover, Alfred Hitchcock, Dorothy Parker, Jacqueline Onassis, Henry Ford, Princess Margaret, and George Bernard Shaw! You've heard of *them*.

Look at him blush with happiness! Ask him to show you his amazing palms. What a fantastic heart line he has! Be on your guard, girls. Have you ever seen a Hill of the Moon like his? Wow! This is some human being!

Which brings us to the arts, whose purpose, in common with astrology, is to use frauds in order to make human beings seem more wonderful than they really are. Dancers show us human beings who move much more gracefully than human beings really move. Films and books and plays show us people talking much more entertainingly than people really talk, make paltry human enterprises seem important. Singers and musicians show us human beings making sounds far more lovely than human beings really make. Architects give us temples in which something marvelous is obviously going on. Actually, practically nothing is going on inside. And on and on.

The arts put man at the center of the universe, whether he belongs there or not. Military science, on the other hand, treats man as garbage—and his children, and his cities, too. Military science is probably right about the contemptibility of man in the vastness of the universe. Still —I deny that contemptibility, and I beg you to deny it, through the creation of appreciation of art.

A friend of mine, who is also a critic, decided to do a paper on things I'd written. He reread all my stuff, which took him about two hours and fifteen minutes, and he was exasperated when he got through. "You know what you do?" he said. "No," I said. "What do I do?" And he said, "You put bitter coatings on very sweet pills."

I would like to do that now, to have the bitterness of my pessimism melt away, leaving you with mouthfuls of a sort of vanilla fudge goo. But I find it harder and harder to prepare confections of this sort—particularly since our military scientists have taken to firing at crowds of their own people. Also—I took a trip to Biafra last January, which was a million laughs. And this hideous war in Indochina goes on and on.

Still—I will give you what goo I have left.

It has been said many times that man's knowledge of himself has been left far behind by his understanding of technology, and that we can have peace and plenty and justice only when man's knowledge of himself catches up. This is not true. Some people hope for great discoveries in the social sciences, social equivalents of $F=ma$ and $E=mc^2$, and so on. Others think we have to evolve, to become better monkeys with bigger brains. We don't need more information. We don't need bigger brains. All that is required is that we become less selfish than we are.

We already have plenty of sound suggestions as to how we are to act if things are to become better on earth. For instance: Do unto others as you would have them do unto you. About seven hundred years ago, Thomas Aquinas had some other recommendations as to what people might do with their lives, and I do not find these made ridiculous by computers and trips to the moon and television sets. He praises the Seven Spiritual Works of Mercy, which are these:

To teach the ignorant, to counsel the doubtful, to console the sad, to reprove the sinner, to forgive the offender, to bear with the oppressive and troublesome, and to pray for us all.

He also admires the Seven Corporal Works of Mercy, which are these:

To feed the hungry, to give drink to the thirsty, to clothe the naked, to shelter the homeless, to visit the sick and prisoners, to ransom captives, and to bury the dead.

A great swindle of our time is the assumption that science has made religion obsolete. All science has damaged is the story of Adam and Eve and the story of Jonah and the Whale. Everything else holds up pretty well, particularly the lessons about fairness and gentleness. People who find those lessons irrelevant in the twentieth century are simply using science as an excuse for greed and harshness.

Science has nothing to do with it, friends.

Another great swindle is that people your age are supposed to save the world. I was a graduation speaker at a little preparatory school for girls on Cape Cod, where I live. I told the girls that they were much too young to save the world and that, after they got their diplomas, they should go swimming and sailing and walking, and just fool around.

I often hear parents say to their idealistic children, "All right, you see so much that is wrong with the world—go out and *do* something about it. We're all *for* you! Go out and *save* the world."

You are four years older than those prep-school girls but still very young. You, too, have been swindled, if people have persuaded you that it is now up to you to save the world. It isn't up to you. You don't have the money and the power. You don't have the appearance of grave maturity—even though you may be gravely mature. You don't even know how to handle dynamite. It is up to older people to save the world. You can help them.

Do not take the entire world on your shoulders. Do a certain amount of skylarking, as befits people your age. "Skylarking," incidentally, used to be a minor offense under Naval Regulations. What a charming crime. It means intolerable lack of seriousness. I would love to have had a dishonorable discharge from the United States Navy —for skylarking not just once, but again and again and again.

Many of you will undertake exceedingly serious work this summer—campaigning for humane Senators and Congressmen, helping the poor and the ignorant and the awfully old. Good. But skylark, too.

When it really is time for you to save the world, when

you have some power and know your way around, when people can't mock you for looking so young, I suggest that you work for a socialist form of government. Free Enterprise is much too hard on the old and the sick and the shy and the poor and the stupid, and on people nobody likes. They just can't cut the mustard under Free Enterprise. They lack that certain something that Nelson Rockefeller, for instance, so abundantly has.

So let's divide up the wealth more fairly than we have divided it up so far. Let's make sure that everybody has enough to eat, and a decent place to live, and medical help when he needs it. Let's stop spending money on weapons, which don't work anyway, thank God, and spend money on each other. It isn't moonbeams to talk of modest plenty for all. They have it in Sweden. We can have it here. Dwight David Eisenhower once pointed out that Sweden, with its many Utopian programs, had a high rate of alcoholism and suicide and youthful unrest. Even so, I would like to see America try socialism. If we start drinking heavily and killing ourselves, and if our children start acting crazy, we can go back to good old Free Enterprise again.

Torture
and
Blubber

HEN I was a young reader of Robin Hood tales and *The White Company* by Arthur Conan Doyle, and so on, I came across the verb "blubber" so often that I looked it up. Bad people in the stories did it when good people punished them hard. It means, of course, to weep noisily and without constraint. No *good* person in a story ever did that.

But it is not easy in real life to make a healthy man blubber, no matter how wicked he may be. So good men have invented appliances which make unconstrained weeping easier—the rack, the boot, the iron maiden, the pediwinkis, the electric chair, the cross, the thumbscrew. And the thumbscrew is alluded to in the published parts of the secret Pentagon history of the Vietnam war. The late Assistant Secretary of Defense, John McNaughton, speaks of each bombing of the North as "... one more turn of the screw."

Simply: We are torturers, and we once hoped to win in Indochina and anywhere because we had the most expensive torture instruments yet devised. I am reminded of the Spanish Armada, whose ships had torture chambers in their holds. Protestant Englishmen were going to be forced to blubber.

The Englishmen refused.

Now the North Vietnamese and the Vietcong have refused. Plenty of them have blubbered like crazy as individuals, God knows—when splattered with jellied gasoline, when peppered with white phosphorus, when crammed into tiger cages and sprinkled with lime. But their societies fight on.

Agony never made a society quit fighting, as far as I know. A society has to be captured or killed—or offered things it values. While Germany was being tortured during the Second World War, with justice, may I add, its industrial output and the determination of its people increased. Hitler, according to Albert Speer, couldn't even be bothered with marveling at the ruins or comforting the survivors. The Biafrans were tortured simultaneously by Nigerians, Russians, and British. Their children starved to death. The adults were skeletons. But they fought on.

One wonders now where our leaders got the idea that mass torture would work to our advantage in Indochina. It never worked anywhere else. They got the idea from childish fiction, I think, and from a childish awe of torture.

Children talk about tortures a lot. They often make up what they hope are new ones. I can remember a friend's saying to me when I was a child: "You want to hear a really neat torture?" The other day I heard a child say to another: "You want to hear a really cool torture?" And then an impossibly complicated engine of pain was described. A cross would be cheaper, and work better, too.

But children believe pain is an effective way to control people, which it isn't—except in a localized, short-term sense. They believe that pain can change minds, which it can't. Now the secret Pentagon history reveals that plenty of high-powered American adults think so, too, some of them college professors. Shame on them for their ignorance.

Torture from the air was the only military scheme open to us, I suppose, since the extermination or capture of the North Vietnamese people would have started World War Three. In which case, *we* would have been tortured from the air.

I am sorry we tried torture. I am sorry we tried anything. I hope we never try torture again. It doesn't work. Human beings are stubborn and brave animals everywhere. They can endure amazing amounts of pain, if they have to. The North Vietnamese and the Vietcong have had to.

Good show.

The American armada to Indochina has been as narrow-minded and futile as the Spanish Armada to England was, though effectively more cruel. Only 27,000 men were involved in the Spanish fiasco. We are said to have more dope addicts than that in Vietnam. Hail, Victory.

Never mind who the American equivalent of Spain's Philip II was. Never mind who lied. Everybody should shut up for a while. Let there be deathly silence as our armada sails home.

Address to the National Institute of Arts and Letters, 1971

I WAS here for the first time last year. My impression then was, "My gosh—how thick the walls are!" (My father was an architect. My grandfather, too.)

When I was invited to give this address, it was explained to me that I need not be serious. I was offended. I hadn't asked permission to be foolish—yet that was what was given to me.

I can be as serious as anyone here, with a few obvious exceptions. And I will prove it. I will speak of happiness, it's true—but I will speak of anthropology and biochemistry and unhappiness as well.

I wish in particular to call your attention to the work of Dr. M. Sydney Margoles, a Los Angeles endocrinologist, who is able to distinguish between male homosexuals and heterosexuals by means of urinalysis. He doesn't even have to meet them. What other sweet mysteries of life are chemicals? All of them, I believe. Biochemistry is everything. The speculations of artists about the human condition are trash.

Happiness is chemical. Before I knew that, I used to investigate happiness by means of questions and answers. (If I had my life to live over, I would learn how to perform a urinalysis.) And I asked my father when he was an old man, "Father—what has been the happiest day in your life so far?"

"It was a Sunday," he said.

Soon after he was married, he said, he bought a new Oldsmobile. This was before the First World War. (The Oldsmobile was not then the tin-knocker's wet dream it has since become.) This was in Indianapolis, Indiana. My father was an architect, as I've said—and a painter, too. And my father, the young architect and painter, took his new wife in his new Oldsmobile to the Indianapolis 500-mile Speedway on a Sunday afternoon. He burglarized a gate. He drove the Oldsmobile onto the track, which was made of bricks. And he and my mother drove around and around and around.

That was a happy day. My father was the widower of a suicide when he told me about that happiest day.

My father told me, too, what he supposed the happiest day in the life of *his* father had been. My paternal grandfather was probably happiest as a boy in Indiana, sitting with a friend on the cowcatcher of a moving locomotive. The locomotive was puffing from Indianapolis to Louisville. There was some wilderness still, and the bridges were made of wood.

When night fell, the sky was filled with fireworks from the stack of the locomotive. What could be nicer than that? Nothing.

My father and grandfather were good artists. I'm sorry they can't be here today. They deserved your warm company in this cool tomb.

(They deserved your cool company in this warm tomb.)

My own son asked me a month ago what the happiest day of my life had been so far. He called down into my grave, so to speak. This speech is *full* of tombs. My son considered me practically dead, since I smoked so many Pall Malls every day. (He's right, too.)

I looked up from the pit, and I told him this: "The happiest day of my life, so far, was in October of 1945. I had just been discharged from the United States Army, which was still an honorable organization in those Walt Disney times. I had just been admitted to the Department of Anthropology of the University of Chicago.

"At last! I was going to study man!"

I began with physical anthropology. I was taught how to measure the size of the brain of a human being who had been dead a long time, who was all dried out. I bored a hole in his skull, and I filled it with grains of polished rice. Then I emptied the rice into a graduated cylinder. I found this tedious.

I switched to archaeology, and I learned something I already knew: that man had been a maker and smasher of crockery since the dawn of time. And I went to my faculty adviser, and I confessed that science did not charm me, that I longed for poetry instead. I was depressed. I knew my wife and my father would want to kill me, if I went into poetry.

My adviser smiled. "How would you like to study poetry which *pretends* to be scientific?" he asked me.

"Is such a thing possible?" I said.

He shook my hand. "Welcome to the field of social or cultural anthropology," he said. He told me that Ruth Benedict and Margaret Mead were already in it—and some sensitive gentlemen as well.

One of those gentlemen was Dr. Robert Redfield, the head of the Department of Anthropology at Chicago. He became the most satisfying teacher in my life. He scarcely noticed me. He sometimes looked at me as though I were a small, furry animal trapped in an office wastebasket. (I stole that image from George Plimpton, by the way. God love him.)

Dr. Redfield is dead now. Perhaps some physical anthropologist of the future will fill his skull with grains of polished rice, and empty it out again—into a graduated cylinder. While he lived, he had in his head a lovely dream which he called "The Folk Society." He published this dream in *The American Journal of Sociology*, Volume 52, 1947, pages 293 through 308.

He acknowledged that primitive societies were bewilderingly various. He begged us to admit, though, that all of them had certain characteristics in common. For instance: They were all so small that everybody knew everybody well, and associations lasted for life. The members communicated intimately with one another, and very little with anybody else.

The members communicated only by word of mouth. There was no access to the experience and thought of the past, except through memory. The old were treasured for their memories. There was little change. What one man knew and believed was the same as what all men knew and believed. There wasn't much of a division of labor. What one person did was pretty much what another person did.

And so on. And Dr. Redfield invited us to call any such society "a Folk Society," a thing I often do. I will now give you a sample of Dr. Redfield's prose, and an opportunity to taste his nostalgia for a sort of society once inhabited by all races of men.

In a folk society, says Dr. Redfield, and I quote him now:

> . . . behavior is personal, not impersonal. A "person" may be defined as that social object which I feel to

respond to situations as I do, with all the sentiments and interests which I feel to be my own; a person is myself in another form, his qualities and values are inherent within him, and his significance for me is not merely one of utility. A "thing," on the other hand, is a social object which has no claim upon my sympathies, which responds to me, as I conceive it, mechanically; its value for me exists in so far as it serves my end. In the folk society, all human beings admitted to the society are treated as persons; one does not deal impersonally ("thing fashion") with any other participant in the little world of that society.

Moreover [Dr. Redfield goes on], in the folk society much besides human beings is treated personally. The pattern of behavior which is first suggested by the inner experience of the individual—his wishes, fears, sensitivities, and interests of all sorts—is projected into all objects with which he comes in contact. Thus nature, too, is treated personally; the elements, the features of the landscape, the animals, and especially anything in the environment which by its appearance or behavior suggests the attributes of mankind—to all these are attributed qualities of the human person. [I stop quoting now.]

And I say to you that we are full of chemicals which require us to belong to folk societies, or failing that, to feel lousy all the time. We are chemically engineered to live in folk societies, just as fish are chemically engineered to live in clean water—and there aren't any folk societies for us anymore.

How lucky you are to be here today, for I can explain *everything*. Sigmund Freud admitted that he did not know

178

what women wanted. I know what they want. *Cosmopolitan* magazine says they want orgasms, which can only be a partial answer at best. Here is what women really want: They want lives in folk societies, wherein everyone is a friendly relative, and no act or object is without holiness. Chemicals make them want that. Chemicals make us all want that.

Chemicals make us furious when we are treated as things rather than persons. When anything happens to us which would not happen to us in a folk society, our chemicals make us feel like fish out of water. Our chemicals demand that we get back into water again. If we become increasingly wild and preposterous in modern times— well, so do fish on river banks, for a little while.

If we become increasingly apathetic in modern times— well, so do fish on river banks, after a little while. Our children often come to resemble apathetic fish—except that fish can't play guitars. And what do many of our children attempt to do? They attempt to form folk societies, which they call "communes." They fail. The generation gap is an argument between those who believe folk societies are still possible and those who know they aren't.

Older persons form clubs and corporations and the like. Those who form them pretend to be interested in this or that narrow aspect of life. Members of the Lions Club pretend to be interested in the cure and prevention of diseases of the eye. They are in fact lonesome Neanderthalers, obeying the First Law of Life, which is this: "Human beings become increasingly contented as they approach the simpleminded, brotherly conditions of a folk society."

The American Academy of Arts and Letters and the National Institute of Arts and Letters don't really give a

179

damn for arts and letters, in my opinion. They, too, are chemically-induced efforts to form a superstitious, affectionate clan or village or tribe. To them I say this, "Lots of luck, boys and girls."

There are other good clubs. The Loyal Order of the Moose is open to any male who is Christian and white. I myself admire The War Dads of America. In order to become a War Dad, one must have had a friend or a relative who served in the armed forces of the United States sometime during the past 195 years. The friend or relative need not have received an honorable discharge, though that helps, I'm told.

It also helps to be stupid. My father and grandfather were not stupid, so they did not join the Moose or anything. They chose solitude instead. Solitude can be nearly as comforting as drugs or fraternities, since there are no other people to remind a solitary person how little like a folk society his society has become. My father had only his young wife with him on his happiest day. My parents were one flesh that day. My grandfather had only a friend with him on his happiest day. There was very little talking— because the locomotive made so much noise.

As for my own happiest day: I was happy because I believed that the Department of Anthropology at the University of Chicago was a small, like-minded family which I was being allowed to join. This was not true.

As I have said before, I can explain *everything* in terms of this biochemical-anthropological theory of mine. Only two men are less mystified by the human condition than

I am today: Billy Graham and Maharishi. If my theory is mistaken, it scarcely matters, since I was told that this need not be a serious speech anyway.

Also, whether I am mistaken or not, we are surely doomed, and so are our artifacts. I have the word of an astronomer on this. Our sun is going to exhaust its fuel eventually. When the heat stops rushing out from its core, our sun will collapse on itself. It will continue to collapse until it is a ball perhaps forty miles in diameter. We could put it between here and Bridgeport.

It will wish to collapse even more, but the atomic nuclei will prevent this. An irresistible force will meet an immovable object, so to speak. There will be a tremendous explosion. Our sun will become a supernova, a flash such as the Star of Bethlehem is thought to have been. Earth Day cannot prevent this.

Somewhere in that flash will be the remains of a 1912 Oldsmobile, a cowcatcher from a locomotive, the University of Chicago, and the paperclip from this year's Blashfield Address.

I thank you.

Reflections
on
My Own
Death

MY Uncle Alex has just calculated in a letter to me that he is a thousand months old, and he told me another time that dying is like a candle's going out. Combustion stops. Uncle Alex is right.

My sister said, just before she died, "No pain." She was surprised. My mother knocked herself off with sleeping pills, which was painless, too. My father thought she had walked out on him. Father was right.

About twenty years after that, my father notified his three children that he was dying of lung cancer, and that it didn't hurt, and that he was serene. It was time, he said.

We were all in the East, and he was in the Middle West, and he sent each one of us a thousand dollars, so we could afford to go back and forth as much as we pleased, while the serene dying was going on.

As it happened, he didn't die until about eighteen months after he mailed the checks. Bill collectors got my sister's money. She was broke, and beginning the process of dying herself, though she didn't know it yet. I invested my thousand dollars in a freight ferry operating between Hyannis and Nantucket—and lost. The boat was declared a menace to navigation. My absentminded brother mislaid his check. Perhaps he's found it again. At any rate, we went back and forth anyway.

And Father died painlessly of what the nurse called "The Old People's Friend," which is pneumonia. And, what the hell, I don't think about death much, unless I'm specifically invited to, which is the case today. I have an actor friend who thinks about death a lot, because that is how he makes himself project mournfulness to an audience when mournfulness is called for onstage. He remembers a dog that died a long time ago. More power to him.

When I think about my own death, I don't console myself with the idea that my descendants and my books and all that will live on. Anybody with any sense knows that the whole solar system will go up like a celluloid collar by-and-by. I honestly believe, though, that we are wrong to think that moments go away, never to be seen again. This moment and every moment lasts forever.

In a Manner That Must Shame God Himself

IF I were a visitor from another planet, I would say things like this about the people of the United States in 1972:

"These are ferocious creatures who imagine that they are gentle. They have experimented in very recent times with slavery and genocide." I would call the robbing and killing of American Indians *genocide*.

I would say, "The two real political parties in America

are the *Winners* and the *Losers.* The people do not acknowledge this. They claim membership in two imaginary parties, the *Republicans* and the *Democrats,* instead.

"Both imaginary parties are bossed by Winners. When Republicans battle Democrats, this much is certain: Winners will win.

"The Democrats have been the larger party in the past —because their leaders have not been as openly contemptuous of Losers as the Republicans have been.

. "Losers can join imaginary parties. Losers can vote."

L osers have thousands of religions, often of the *bleeding heart* variety," I would go on. "The single religion of the Winners is a harsh interpretation of *Darwinism*, which argues that it is the will of the universe that only the fittest should survive.

"The most pitiless Darwinists are attracted to the Republican party, which regularly purges itself of suspected *bleeding hearts.* It is in the process now of isolating and ejecting Representative Paul N. McCloskey, for instance, who has openly raged and even wept about the killing and maiming of Vietnamese.

"The Vietnamese are impoverished farmers, far, far away. The Winners in America have had them bombed and shot day in and day out, for years on end. This is not madness or foolishness, as some people have suggested. It is a way for the Winners to learn how to be pitiless. They understand that the material resources of the planet are almost exhausted, and that pity will soon be a form of suicide.

"The Winners are rehearsing for *Things to Come.*"

In a Manner That Must Shame God Himself

There is a witty winner, a millionaire named William F. Buckley, Jr.," I would go on, "who appears regularly in newspapers and on television. He bickers amusingly with people who think that Winners should help the Losers more than they do.

"He has a nearly permanent and always patronizing rictus when debating."

As a visitor from another planet, I would have nothing to lose socially in supposing that Buckley himself did not know the secret message of his smile. I would then guess at the message: "Yes, oh yes, my dear man—I understand what you have said so clumsily. But you know in your heart what every Winner knows: that one must behave heartlessly toward Losers, if one hopes to survive."

That may not really be the message in the Buckley smile. But I guarantee you that it was the monolithic belief that underlay the Republican National Convention in Miami Beach, Florida, in 1972.

All the rest was hokum.

Listen: I went to a private luncheon for Winners in Miami Beach, while the convention was farting around several miles away. Nelson Rockefeller was there. John Kenneth Galbraith was there. William F. Buckley, Jr., was there. Arthur O. Sulzberger was there. Jacob Javits was there. Clare Boothe Luce was there. Art Buchwald was there. Barbara Walters was there. Everybody was there. Whether one was a Republican or a Democrat was a hilarious accident, which nobody was required to explain.

I asked Dr. Galbraith what he was doing at a Republican convention. He replied that he had been offered an *indecent* amount of money to banter with Buckley in the morning on NBC.

Barbara Walters invited me to appear on the *Today* show. I told her that I had nothing to say. The convention had left me speechless. It was so heavily guarded, spiritually and physically, that I hadn't been able to see or hear anything that wasn't already available in an official press release. "It's Disneyland under martial law," I said.

"You don't have to say much," she said.

"I'd have to say *something*," I said.

"Just say, 'hello,' " she said.

Hello.

Art Buchwald said he came to the convention in order to see his pals, mostly other news people. He told our table about a column he had just written. The comical premise was that the Republican party had attracted so many campaign contributions that it found itself with two billion dollars it couldn't spend. It decided to buy something nice for the American people. Here was the gift: a free week's bombing of Vietnam.

I asked Clare Boothe Luce what she thought of some young people's efforts to stimulate pity for the people of Vietnam. They had been dressing as Vietnamese there in Miami Beach, and carrying dolls that were painted to look as though they had been disemboweled and burned alive and so on.

Mrs. Luce wished the young people would take an automobile and fill it with something resembling blood. She said she had lost two members of her family in automobile accidents. Automobiles were easily the most terrible killers of our times, she said. Young people should protest about them.

In a Manner That Must Shame God Himself

As for the Nixon versus McGovern thing: Everybody was sure that Nixon would win. McGovern, I gathered, though nobody said so out loud, was the butt of a rather elegant practical joke. He was a Winner who had been encouraged by other Winners to identify himself with Losers, to bury himself up to his neck in the horseshit of Populism, so to speak.

Losers hate to vote for Losers. They know what Losers are.

So Nixon would win.

What remained to be discovered at the convention was, among other things, how much pity Republicans as individuals felt for the Vietnamese, and for Americans who were badly housed and badly nourished and so on.

The scientific conclusion is that there was a satisfactory level of pity when the delegates were ordinary social creatures, more or less in isolation and at rest, when majestic policies were not being promulgated in thundering meetings, when the delegates were not threatened by hostile crowds.

But there was a Pavlovian thing going on, and it has been going on for many years now: The wishes of the hostile crowds were invariably humanitarian, and the crowds weren't even hostile most of the time. But wherever they went, armies of policemen went too—to protect nice people from them.

So a Pavlovian connection has been made in the minds of people who are really awfully nice: When more than two people show up with a humanitarian idea, the police should be called.

If the police don't act immediately, and if the humanitarians behave in a manner that is dignified or beautiful or heartbreaking, there is still something nice people can do.

They can ignore the humanitarians.

This is what the nice people did when one of the most honorable military reviews in American history took place on the afternoon of August 22, 1972, in front of the Hotel Fontainebleau. This date will not go down in history, because nice people do not want it there.

Several hundred American gunfighters, killers from the war in Vietnam, formed themselves into platoons, with the proper intervals between the platoons. Many wore the raffish, spooky rags of modern jungle warfare. They marched silently, in the slope-shouldered route step of tired, hungry veterans—which they were. Their hair was often long, which gave them the cavalier beauty of Indian killers from another time.

Some were in wheelchairs. Many had wounds. John Wayne, the gunfighter's gunfighter, was in Miami Beach somewhere. But he was nowhere to be seen when these real gunfighters came to town. Here was Billy the Kid, multiplied by a thousand—not even whispering, and formed into platoons before the Fontainebleau.

They sat down silently, which was a crime. They were blocking a public thoroughfare. Some sighed. Some scratched themselves.

Their message was this: "Let the killing stop."

They went home again.

How many nice people came out of the hotel or came to hotel windows to watch them? None—almost none. It was a police affair.

In a Manner That Must Shame God Himself

As for the nonsensical business to be performed by run-of-the-mill delegates: It was mostly listening to speeches composed of glittering half-truths, of listening to eminent theologians pray, of getting autographs, of recoiling from hostile crowds. Saul Steinberg, the most intelligent artist of our time, should have covered it for *The New Yorker,* along with Renata Adler and Richard Rovere.

It was all clouds and curlicues.

As for the prayers: I heard a lot of famous Republicans and eminent theologians pray at a Worship Service on the Sunday before the convention began. That is another date I would like to see go into American history books: August 20, 1972. In a moment, I will explain why it belongs there.

I listened closely to all the preaching and praying. I wanted to learn, if I could, what the Republican God was shaped like. I came away with this impression: He was about the size of Mount Washington, and very slow to anger.

There were a lot of little sermons, but the main one was delivered, at the request of Richard M. Nixon himself, by Dr. D. Elton Trueblood, a Quaker philosopher, Professor at Large of Earlham College in Richmond, Indiana. Earlham, like Whittier College where Mr. Nixon went to school, is a Quaker school.

Dr. Trueblood's sermon surprised me at one point, because I thought I heard him say that the sovereignty exercised by American politicians came directly from God. Some other reporters there got the same impression. He was speaking extemporaneously, so no copies of the sermon were made available for a detailed check.

But I interviewed him afterward, and recorded our conversation, which went like this:

"After your sermon this morning," I said, "I heard someone say that you had traced sovereignty from the President directly to God. We are usually taught that the sovereignty of the President resides in the people. I was wondering, since you are a theologian—"

"I said nothing about the President," said Trueblood. "I said the sovereignty is God's, not ours, that all we do is under Judgment. This is a way to have a nonidolatrous patriotism."

"So the circuitry would go like this," I said, "if we were to lay it out like a wiring diagram: The President draws his sovereignty from the people, and the people draw it from God. Is that it?"

"No," he said. "I would put it another way: that God alone is sovereign. I accept Luther's doctrine of the two kingdoms of the Church and State, both under God. So that everything we do as a state is under Judgment, therefore derivative."

"So the President is simultaneously responsible to the people and to God?"

"But even more to God than to the people, of course," Dr. Trueblood replied.

I set this down so meticulously and without elisions because I think it proves my claim that on August 20, 1972, the Republican National Convention was opened with a sermon on the *Divine Right of Presidents.*

Of water commissioners too.

I told Dr. Trueblood that I thought Quakers were pacifists and that I was startled by the energy with which

Richard M. Nixon, who had a Quaker background, could prosecute a war.

He said I had a simplistic notion about what Quakerism was, that a lot of Americans did. "Why," he said, "when I go around on speaking engagements, they all expect me to look like the man on the box of Quaker Oats."

"So, at this stage of American history, Quakers are an awful lot like everybody else?" I suggested.

Dr. Trueblood agreed heartily. "And we are just as mixed up as everybody else," he assured me. "And anybody that believes in a single pattern of Quaker, he is just plain stupid."

I said to him that many peace-loving people must know that he had the ear of the President and that they must have told him, "My God, Dr. Trueblood, tell him to stop the war."

"Yes," he said, "and often in a most nasty mood, very judgmental sometimes. And I say to them, 'Look here, he is trying to stop it. Don't hinder him in your self-righteousness.' I don't take any lip off them, you understand."

And this Quaker philosopher had even heavier news than that for the bleeding hearts. He was about to send to the President a little-known quotation from Abraham Lincoln, with whom Mr. Nixon in his wartime anguish identifies.

This was it:

> We are indeed going through a great trial, a fiery trial. In the very responsible position in which I happen to be placed, being an humble instrument in the hands of our Heavenly Father, as I am and as we all are, to work out His great purposes I have decided that all my works and acts may be according to His Will.

And, that it might be so, I have sought His aid.

But if, after endeavoring to do my best in the life which He affords me, I find my efforts fail, I must believe that, for some purpose unknown to me, He wills it otherwise.

If I had my way, this war would never have been commenced. If I had been allowed my way, this war would have ended before this. But we find that it still continues, and we must believe that He permits it for some wise purpose of His Own, mysterious and unknown to us; and though, with our limited understanding, we are not able to comprehend it, yet we cannot but believe that He Who made the world still governs it.

I hate to think of this document's falling into the President's hands. I am persuaded that Mr. Nixon, in his splendid humorlessness, does not understand that he is implementing the harsh, long-term survival plans of the Winners as opposed to the Losers, of the fat people versus the thin. It seems entirely possible to me, now that I have learned for sure that his spiritual advisers are so appallingly commonplace, that he honestly believes that he is serving God, no matter what he does.

If I were a visitor from another planet, by the way, here is how I would explain Mr. Nixon's actual malice toward Losers: I would say that it was because his family was poor during the Great Depression and it was a humiliation to them to be lumped with other poor people. It was as though the Nixons had all been locked up in a dog pound by mistake.

In a Manner That Must Shame God Himself

The President now demonstrates that he can't stand anything about the poor people with whom he was so unjustly associated so long ago.

The Republicans were as high as kites at their convention, of course, since victory was a certainty. The enemy candidate was buried up to his neck in Populism, whereas their own candidate was buried up to his neck in God. Nothing remained to be done, so autographing parties starring the President's wife and daughters loomed large on the official schedules for every day.

These pleasant, pretty women were modest and shy. They seemed to say with body language: "You should be getting the autographs of some of the really famous movie stars around." Who were some of the really famous movie stars at the convention? Well, Ethel Merman was one.

So I stepped out of an elevator at the Fontainebleau on the third day of the convention. I myself was now giving out autographs. I had actually given one to a rioter while a riot was going on. I was also building a respectable collection of prayers and sermons. I had just picked up a mimeographed copy of what George G. Seibels, Jr., the mayor of Birmingham, Alabama, had said on the same program with Dr. Trueblood on Sunday.

Mayor Seibels himself had just handed it to me, and it was all written in capital letters.

I AM DEEPLY GRATEFUL THAT YOU ACCORD ME THIS SIGNAL HONOR IN BRINGING YOU A MESSAGE, "ONE NATION UNDER GOD" [it began], A SUBJECT

Kurt Vonnegut, Jr.

VERY DEAR TO ME AND MILLIONS OF OTHER AMERI-
CANS OF ALL CREEDS, COLORS, AND RACES. SO AP-
PROPRIATE IT IS THAT ON THIS SABBATH DAY WE
COMMENCE OUR CONVENTION ACTIVITIES WITH
THIS WORSHIP SERVICE.

I now accosted one of the hundreds of nubile girls who
had flown to Miami at their own expense. They were living
proof that young people were crazy about Mr. Nixon. I
had heard them cry out their admiration for Ethel Merman at a party for celebrities and youth on the afternoon
before.

"I am from *Harper's* magazine," I said, "and I would
like to ask you if you think an atheist could possibly be a
good President of the United States."

"I don't see how," she said.

"Why not?" I said.

"Well—" she said, "this whole country is founded on
God."

"Could a Jew be a good President?" I asked.

"I don't know enough about that to say," she replied.

This was a beautiful white child. I tore my eyes away
from her reluctantly, and what did I see? I saw ten American Indians sitting all by themselves on overstuffed furniture in the lobby. Nine were big male Indians.

One was an Indian boy.

Those Indians seemed to have turned to redwood. They
did not talk. They did not swivel their heads around to see
who was who.

They had a coffee table all to themselves. On it were
mimeographed copies of a message they had come great
distances to deliver. They were from many tribes.

In a Manner That Must Shame God Himself

As I would later discover, the message was addressed as follows: "Att'n: Richard M. Nixon, President U.S.A." The message said this in part:

> We come today in such a manner that must shame God himself. For a country which allows a complete body of people to exist in conditions which are at variance with the ideals of this country, conditions which daily commit injustices and inhumanity, must surely be filled with hate, greed, and unconcern.

I did not go directly to the Indians. I chatted first with a reporter friend. He told me a thing that Dr. Daniel Ellsberg, who had made the Pentagon Papers public, had said about Dr. Henry Kissinger, the President's strikingly happy adviser on foreign affairs. This was it: "Henry has the best deal Faust ever made with Mephistopheles."

I thought that was a ravishing remark. Ellsberg was at the convention, incidentally. Nobody seemed to notice him, even though he stood for everything good Republicans considered treacherous and vile. This was because he looked so much like just another security man.

I told my friend that I had watched Dr. Kissinger on television, while he made gifts of Dutch uncle smiles and autographs to a pair of little girls in white organdy. I was glad that Ellsberg brought up the subject of Mephistopheles, because the the scene had seemed definitely evil to me.

Little girls represent life at its most playful and promising, I said. And anybody in Dr. Kissinger's job had a lot to do with random, pointless deaths in Vietnam these days

197

—even deaths of little girls in white on our side. So evil came with the job. Under the circumstances, I found it ugly that a man in such a job would give out Dutch uncle smiles and autographs.

I now glimpsed Abbie Hoffman, the clowning revolutionary. He had been stopped for perhaps the dozenth time that day by security men, who looked just like Dr. Ellsberg. He was a weary clown by now. His press credentials were in order. He was gathering material for a book.

"Who you representing?" he was asked.

"Field and Stream," he said.

I had the feeling he wasn't going to be clowning much more. A lot of naturally funny people who want to help Losers aren't going to clown anymore. They have caught on that clowning doesn't throw off the timing or slow down cruel social machinery. In fact, it usually serves as a lubricant.

Every so often somebody tells me that it is a delicious fact of history that clowns have often been the most effective revolutionaries. That isn't true. Cruel social machines in the past have needed clowns for lubrication so much that they have often manufactured them. Consider the Spanish Inquisition.

When the Inquisition was about to burn somebody alive in a public square, it shaved that person from head to foot. It tortured the person to the point of babbling idiocy, fitted him out with a dunce cap and a lurid paper cloak. His or her face was painted or masked.

Hey presto! A clown!

The idea, of course, was to make the victim comical

rather than pitiful. Pity is like rust to a cruel social machine.

I do not say that America's Winners are about to burn America's Losers in public squares—although, if they did, it would be nothing new. I say that the Winners are avid to *neglect* the Losers, which is cruelty too.

And neglecting becomes easier, if only the victims or people who seem to represent them will look like clowns. If clownish-looking people hadn't come to Miami Beach to raise hell with the convention, there still would have been plenty of clowns in the cartoons and prose in campaign literature floating around—jackbooted lesbians, mincing male homosexuals, drug-crazed hippies, prostitutes on their way to the unemployment office in Cadillacs, big fat black mamas with thirteen children and no papa around.

News item from *First Monday,* an official party publication:

> Yippie leader Jerry Rubin, a backer of Sen. George McGovern, "no longer" believes that people should kill their parents to demonstrate their dedication to change.

And so on.

And those Indians in the lobby of the Fontainebleau were moving so little, were saying so little because their people were dying of neglect, and they knew damn well that even if they sneezed, this would allow some people to dismiss them as clowning redskins.

So now they were in danger of becoming comical because of their petrified dignity.

These Indians had been harrowingly defeated by white men in greedy, unjust wars. They had been offered death or unconditional surrender—death, or life under hideous conditions. Those who had chosen life, which some people think is a holy thing, asked for mercy now. Their average life expectancy was only forty-six years. Their babies died with sickening regularity. Their water rights had been stolen. Some of their best men were woozy with tuberculosis and narcotics and booze. Their government-run schools were indifferent to Indian ideas of holiness, and so were the white man's laws of the land. One of the things the Indians had come to beg from President Nixon, who never begged anything from anybody, was that their religions be recognized as respectable religions under law.

As the law now stands, they told me, their religions are negligible superstitions deserving no respect.

I'll say this: Their religions couldn't possibly be more chaotic than the Christianity reinvented every day by Dr. D. Elton Trueblood, Professor at Large.

The Indian I talked to most was Ron Petite, a Chippewa. He said that he and the others had come from all over the country to Flamingo Park in Miami Beach, where Losers and friends of Losers had caused a tent city to be built. They moved right out again, disgusted and frightened by clowns.

They went to the Hollywood Indian Reservation, a few miles north of Miami, where Indian notions of sacredness and dignity were respected. They would not be represented there by some hairy white youth who was willing to set a flag on fire and piss on it as a surrogate for oppressed people everywhere.

Ron Petite told a very funny Indian story without cracking a smile. He and the others came into the Fontainebleau with their message to Mr. Nixon, and nobody of any importance would take it from them. They were ignored.

But then they saw people forming into lines. The President's daughters were going to give out autographs. So the Indians got into line too, and patiently waited their turn. Indians are legendary for patience.

When they arrived at last before Patricia or Julie—they weren't sure which—they gave her a message for Dad.

And her dad would say in his acceptance speech that night, among other things, "We covet no one else's territory. We seek no dominion over any other people. We seek peace not only for ourselves but for all the peoples in the world." This was what he had said on Russian television in May.

As a visitor from another planet, I would have to say that this was only kind of true. I think of all the Winners at that private party for Winners I went to, and how they like to live, and what good care they take of their financial affairs. They want to go anywhere on the planet and live however they please, buy whatever they please.

What could be more human than that?

They want to be planetary aristocrats, welcomed everywhere. Again: What could be more human than that?

What seems to charm them as much as anything about the rapprochement with China is that they may soon be able to travel there again. That charms *me* too.

If we really liked some part of China, we might want to put up a little house there, or a motel—or a Colonel Sanders Kentucky Fried Chicken franchise.

We don't covet anybody's territory. We would just like to buy or rent some of it, if we can—and then everybody can get rich.

If I were a visitor from another planet, radioing home about Earth. I wouldn't call Americans *Americans.* I would give them a name that told a lot about them immediately: I would call them *Realtors.*

I would call the Republicans *Super Realtors.* I would call the Democrats *Inferior Realtors.* And one thing that fascinated me about the Super Realtors' Worship Service on Sunday was that Colonel Frank Borman was on the bill. He looked as tired of space opera as Abbie Hoffman was of clowning. He did his bit, which was to read about the Creation from *Genesis,* and that was that.

At no point in the Super Realtors' Convention was there any Kennedy-style boosterism about the glorious opportunities for Americans in outer space.

Since there were plenty of Republicans at the convention who were dumb enough to believe that McGovern was really an enthusiast for acid, amnesty, and abortion, I am free to think that they were dumb enough at one point to hope that nice properties might be had for a song on the Moon.

They had sent some good Republicans up there to have a look around, to cancel some stamps, to pray and hit a few golf balls, and they knew better now. Not even Losers, with all their lazy resourcefulness, could survive on the Moon.

So it was time to think hardheaded thoughts about efficient use of the surface of the Earth again.

And why not make friends again with our old friends the Chinese?

I t was perhaps unkind of me to associate Dr. Kissinger with evil. That is no casual thing to do in a country as deeply religious as ours is.

As the mayor of Birmingham told us about our nation on Sunday,

WITH ALL OUR LABORS, SUCCESS OR FAILURE, NOW
AND IN THE YEARS AHEAD IT WILL, GOD WILLING,
ALWAYS BE "ONE NATION UNDER GOD."

Dr. Kissinger, after all, has been a healer of terrible wounds between the mightiest nations of all. But the Administration he serves is bad news for those nations that are feeble, or what the King James version of the Bible calls "the meek."

The Super Realtors, with Dr. Kissinger as their representative, have worked out crude agreements with the few other truly terrifying powers of the planet as to what can be done and what must not be done with the real estate of the meek.

The Nixon-Kissinger scheme, the Winners' scheme, the neo-Metternichian scheme for lasting world peace is simple. Its basic axiom is to be followed by individuals as well as great nations, by Losers and Winners alike. We have demonstrated the workability of the axiom in Vietnam, in

Bangladesh, in Biafra, in Palestinian refugee camps, in our own ghettos, in our migrant labor camps, on our Indian reservations, in our institutions for the defective and the deformed and the aged.

This is it: *Ignore agony.*

I might, with justice and no irony, call Americans *Healers* instead of *Realtors.* I spoke to Art Linkletter at the convention, and he is profoundly bent on healing, and he is as typical an American as one could find.

He had visited South Korea recently, he said, where he had worked years ago to heal children hurt by warfare. They were healthy, happy men and women now. And he had gone to Vietnam too, to help the children with fresher wounds.

(And I must digress at this point to coin an acronym that can serve me now, which is "JACFU." A similar acronym, "JANFU," was coined during the Second World War, along with "SNAFU." It meant "Joint Army-Navy Fuck-Up." I would like "JACFU" to mean "Joint American-Communist Fuck-Up.")

And the children Art Linkletter and so many other Americans are mending or want to mend are surely victims of JACFU.

The walking wounded within our own boundaries, our undeserving poor, are not by any stretch of the imagination victims of JACFU. We creamed them ourselves. Money is tight. We can only afford to heal them a little bit; and even that little bit hurts Winners like bloody murder.

In a Manner That Must Shame God Himself

My close friend Dexter Leen, who is a shoe merchant in Hyannis on Cape Cod, used to read *The New York Times* every Sunday, and then come over to my house and tell me that, on the basis of what he had read in there, things were slowly but surely getting better all the time. I remember talking to him one time too, about awful automobile drivers we had known. He knew one woman, back in the days when all cars had radiator ornaments, who never took her eyes off her radiator ornament, he said.

And looking at one day's news or a few days' news or a few years' news is a lot like staring at the radiator ornament of a Stutz Bearcat, it seems to me. Which is why so many of us would love to have a visitor from another planet, who might have a larger view of our day-to-day enterprises, who might be able to give us some clue as to what is really going on.

He would tell us, I think, that no real Winner fears God or believes in a punitive afterlife. He might say that Earthlings put such emphasis on truthfulness in order to be believed when they lie. President Nixon, for instance, was free to lie during his acceptance speech at the convention, if he wanted to, because of his famous love for the truth. And the name of the game was "Survival." Everything else was hokum.

He might congratulate us for learning so much about healing the planet, and warn us against wounding the planet so horribly during our real estate dealings, that it might never heal.

The visitor might say by way of farewell what Charles Darwin seemed to say to us, and we might write his words in stone, all in capital letters, like the words of the mayor of Birmingham:

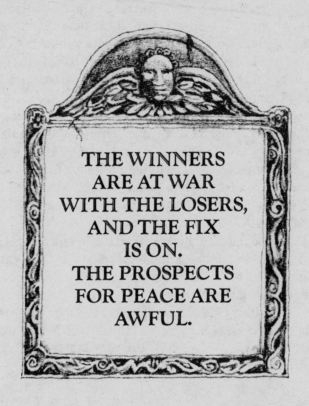

THE WINNERS
ARE AT WAR
WITH THE LOSERS,
AND THE FIX
IS ON.
THE PROSPECTS
FOR PEACE ARE
AWFUL.

Thinking
Unthinkable,
Speaking
Unspeakable

THE prohibition of the sale of alcoholic beverages in this country was called "The Noble Experiment," among other things. It did a lot to destroy our respect for policemen, who were expected to enforce laws which were stupid and unpopular. The war in Vietnam might aptly be called "Noble Experiment II," since it is a similarly narrow-minded adventure in virtue. It has left us with a secret and unjust contempt for our soldiers, especially our airmen. That contempt will become less and less secret as time goes by.

People think unthinkable things and speak unspeakable things in the privacy of their homes, meaning no harm when blurting this or that. And a reasonable woman said to me in such privacy a few days ago that she couldn't really care what happened to some of our prisoners of war. She pitied the captured ground soldiers and the captured fliers who had flown in support of troops. But she thought that the fliers who were shot down while bombing civilians from the stratosphere shouldn't have been doing what they were doing. "I wouldn't want to wear a bracelet with one of their names on it, and pray for his early return to his family and all that," she said. "I'm sorry."

I reminded her that the fliers could be given prison terms for refusing to bomb this or that. "They could have resigned," she said. We had seen films of recently captured airmen on television the night before, and she didn't think they were noble or anything. "They volunteered," she said. "They didn't have to do that. They're healthy and intelligent, and the country is prosperous. There are plenty of things they could have done in civilian life."

And so on.

"If I were Joan Baez," she said, "I wouldn't have gone over there to give them Christmas presents and sing them songs."

So, in the privacy of her home, she was no longer able to believe in a romance which in the past has made us so energetic when defending our soldiers—the romance of their being innocent soldier boys.

We have made our soldiers ghastly by giving them ghastly things to do.

Too bad.

Some experiment.

Noble Experiment I, which was Prohibition, gave us a hardy and heartless new class, the gangster businessmen, who can be expected to sicken our society for at least another hundred years. I am curious to see if Noble Experiment II will leave us with a similarly persistent disease. We encouraged and admired the gangsters when they were getting their start, and it seems possible to me that we may now encourage mercenary warriors in our midst. That is how I would write it, if I were writing science fiction.

There would be this jaded, cynical country, see, where romance was dead as a doornail, and it would create this ferocious, highly paid warrior class. And so on. And the next thing the people knew. . . .

And so on.

I don't really think that will happen. I do think, though, that we will continue to elect priggish, ignorant, stubborn people to high office. Their blind enthusiasms, commonly learned at their mothers' knees, will lead us into more noble experiments.

Humanity will again fail to cooperate—because the experiments will be incomprehensible to most human beings, and painful and wasteful besides. Humanity will come to look like a defective machine to the noble experimenters. They will order our policemen and soldiers to bang on it hard, to make it run smoothly.

The experimenters will again force our policemen and soldiers to disgrace themselves in public. Sorry about that.

Address at Rededication of Wheaton College Library, 1973

I CONGRATULATE
this beloved college for having a library. If a teacher forgets something, he or she doesn't have to pretend he or she still knows it. He or she can come to the library and look it up, or he or she can force a student to look it up. Nobody has to fake facts at Wheaton, unless he or she is too lazy to live.

The burning of the library of Wheaton would not be the

intellectual catastrophe that the burning of the library of Alexandria, Egypt, was. There were no duplicates of many of the books at Alexandria. Our civilization has since developed a mania for duplication. Because there are so many duplicates of everything, our culture can be said to be fireproof.

I think we can say without fear of contradiction, too, that our books are not as full of baloney as many of the lost books of Alexandria were. People in those days believed all sorts of things which simply were not true. Those were pitiful days.

The Alexandrians believed that the World was the center of the Universe. They didn't know that teeny-weeny little animals and unhappy childhoods caused a lot of disease. They fought with knives. That's all in your library here—what those people were like. We're in there, too. New books about us arrive every day. What are we like? We are a mixture of good and evil.

I am fascinated by the good and evil in myself and in everyone, and I can't get anybody to talk about either one anymore. People are embarrassed for me.

I am fascinated by the good and evil in your library.

As for goodness: Members of my generation in America had the illusion of being very, very good during the Second World War. This was because we were engaged in a just war. Most people never have that exhilarating experience. Almost every war ends, properly, with its veterans feeling deceived and pointless and gullible, with their being persuaded that all participants were equally vile. It wasn't so with American veterans in World War Two—and British veterans and Canadian veterans and Australian veterans and Frenchmen who had fought on our side—and so on. We would have said the Nazis were evil in any event, since we had decided to fight them. That has always been the style in war, until very recently, anyhow: to declare the enemy evil—in order that we can be frenzied on the battlefield. Imagine our surprise when we discovered that our German enemies really were satanic this time. They had been accused of making soap and candles out of human beings in the First World War. They really did it in the second one. We had fought something which was totally obscene.

This was very bad for us. We were empty-headed children in that war, as all ground soldiers are. Anything could be put in our heads and we would believe it. And one idea that was put into our heads was that our enemies were so awful, so evil, that we, by contrast, must be remarkably pure. That illusion of purity, to which we were entitled in a way, has become our curse today. And I celebrate your having a library because it is the memory of mankind. It reminds us that all human beings are to a certain extent impure.

To put it another way: All human beings are to some extent greedy and cruel—and angry without cause. Here I am, due to become fifty years old two days from now. I have imagined during most of that half century that I was responding to life around me as a just and sensitive man, blowing my cork with good reason from time to time. Only recently, with the help of a physician, have I realized that I have blown my cork every twenty days, no matter what is really going on. I become cruel—and I become angry without cause. This is the evil in me. Lest I make some of you nervous, let me assure you that Vesuvius is not due to erupt for another six days.

I am not pure. We are not pure. Our nation is not pure. And I insist that at the core of the American tragedy, best

213

exemplified by the massacre of civilians at My Lai, is the illusion engendered by World War Two: that in the war between good and evil we are always, perfectly naturally, on the side of good. This is what makes us so unrestrained in the uses of weaponry.

We trust ourselves so much with weapons that many American households keep firearms as pets. Too many of us treat guns with genial familiarity. Guns should give us the heebie-jeebies. They are killing machines. That is *all* they are. We should dread them the way we dread cancer and cyanide and electric chairs.

My father collected guns. He kept them oiled. He traded them with other gun nuts—those man-killing machines. This was his way of proving to Indianapolis, Indiana, that he wasn't a pansy, even though he was in the arts: He was an architect. I simply left Indianapolis, which is a big improvement on spitting into corners and collecting guns. And what does this have to do with the library at Wheaton? Well, among other things, there are a lot of gun stories in there, both history books and novels about the creative use of explosives and firearms.

It may be that such mind-rotting histories and novels have as much to do with American character flaws as did World War Two. I am not competent to represent historians who have focused on the evolution of human violence, on how wars were lost or won. I can represent fiction writers, though, and I want to apologize for all of us. We have ended so many of our stories with gunfights, with showdowns and death, and millions upon millions of simpletons have mistaken our stories for models for modern living. We have ended our stories with showdowns and death so often because we're so lazy. Gunplay is no way to live—but it's a peachy way to end a tale. It became more than the end of story after story to Lee Harvey Oswald and Sirhan Sirhan and Arthur Bremer, to name a few. To the likes of them, it became the most compelling myth, most ennobling moral lesson of our times.

What other damage have storytellers done? Well—again—they did it innocently, and they were simply trying to solve certain technical problems inherent in their craft. The shoot-out was a way to end a story, a hard thing to do. Another thing that was hard to do was to hold the attention of a reader or watcher for any length of time. It was discovered that audiences had an easier time of it if they didn't have to care equally about all the characters in a tale. So storytellers provided plots with characters whose destinies mattered a lot, and other characters who were as disposable as Kleenex tissues. This, too, was taken as a model for life by certain dumb bunnies. A heartbreaking example of this confusion of stories with real life was the indiscriminate butchery of bit-part players during the prison uprising at Attica, New York. All leading characters were elsewhere, so State Police with automatic shotguns blazing could be sent in without harming the play.

What other crazy ideas have we accidentally put in people's heads? A lot of dumbbells think we put sex in there. We are innocent of the charge. The blame belongs elsewhere. I name no names. My mother-in-law wrote me a long time ago from an apartment house for moderately prosperous widows in Indianapolis, where she lived. She asked me to stop putting dirty words in my books—on economic grounds. She said she understood that I hoped

215

to sell a lot of books because of the dirty words, but that exactly the opposite effect had been achieved—in her apartment building, at least. The dirty words were stopping her friends from buying my books. In the book she was talking about, I had had American soldiers talk as American soldiers talk, and I was glad to be free to do so.

On some level, I suppose I enjoyed the freedom to shock a few old ladies, too. And, ten or more years ago now, when students and some authors were insisting on the right to use any damn words they pleased, this was perceived by many easily frightened people as a form of assault. They were right. The primary wish of many free-speech fanatics was, I am certain, to bop prudes around. That's always fun. But something beautiful came out of the legalization of all the funny, endearing, ugly little words. We were not only free to mention any part of our bodies we damn pleased, thus improving our mental health and our understanding of ourselves to the extent that we are machines. We were free to discuss anything! When I learned politeness at my mother's knee—God rest her soul, God rest her knee—I learned not to offend anyone by discussing excretion, reproduction, religion, or a person's sources of wealth. We are free to discuss all those things now. Our minds aren't crippled anymore by good taste. And I can see now all the other more sinister taboos which mingled with sexuality and excretion, such as religious hypocrisy and ill-gotten wealth. If we are to discuss truthfully what America is and what it can become, our discussion must be in absolutely rotten taste, or we won't be discussing it at all.

I suppose that writers have squirreled away communistic ideas in your library here and there. They'll do that, given half a chance. They'll hide them around like Easter eggs. I myself yearn for a fairer sharing of work and wealth. "From each according to his abilities. To each according to his needs." What could be more American than that? What could be more puritanical than that? It would be a bewilderingly appropriate message to carve into Plymouth Rock.

But I am not a Marxist or a Maoist, either. I am in the arts, and my closest friends are in the arts, and under either Marxism or Maoism, or under any sort of monolithic dictatorship, we would all be creamed. I do not want to be creamed. Unlike some of my colleagues, I don't expect America to cream me by and by. This is a conservative nation. It continues to do what it has always done, for good or evil. It will continue to treat nonwhite people badly. It has always done that. It will continue to let its writers run free, no matter what they say. It has always done that. It's lazy about change. I'm lucky to be the color I am and to do what I do. This is the place for me.

As for schemes to make America better than it is, this much I've figured out: Large families in stable neighborhoods take better care of their members than the Government can. As for this last election: I was on McGovern's side, and we deserved to lose.

It isn't the end of the world here. It could be the end of the world in Vietnam. I think every human being has a potential for greatness. It seems entirely possible to me that Richard Nixon, as a lame duck, can become a great man. He must suppress the evil in himself, which is to say his unconstitutionality. So must we all. *

Kurt Vonnegut, Jr.

William F. Buckley said in a recent column that I would be overjoyed by Nixon's political defeat, since I had made a career of despising America. That proves he hasn't read me much. He said, too, that I made money out of talking of love. Actually, I am highly suspicious of love, and any honest biography of me would bear that out. If somebody says, "I love you," to me, I feel as though I had a pistol pointed at my head. What can anybody reply under such conditions but that which the pistol-holder requires? "I love you, *too*." The hell with love, and hooray for something else, which I can't even begin to name or describe.

About good and evil again—and your library. The books and the films and the records and the tapes and the pictures you have in there have come from the best parts of human beings who have often, in real life, been contemptible in many ways. The best example I know of goodness from vileness is the body of humane writings produced by Louis-Ferdinand Céline, a French physician and novelist, who was a convicted war criminal after World War Two. Louis-Ferdinand Céline was his pen name. His real name was Louis-Ferdinand Destouches. He was the son of poor people. He spent most of his adult life as a badly paid physician who treated the poor. I read his early novels without knowing anything about his vicious anti-Semitism. He kept it out of his early books. The internal evidence of those books persuaded me, and many others, too, that I was in the presence of a great man.

I was in fact in the presence of greatness in a man—the goodness he could find when ransacking himself. So be it.

Address at Rededication of Wheaton College Library, 1973

He is dead now. I love the good part of him. He died of natural causes. He died on July 1, 1961. Curiously—Ernest Hemingway shot himself on the very same day.

Thus ends my speech. I thank you.

Invite
Rita
Rait to
America!

I WANT Rita Rait
(pronounced *Wright*) to be invited to the United States by
our Government and by some of our universities as soon
as possible. She is the champion and translator in the
Soviet Union of William Faulkner and J. D. Salinger and
John Updike and Franz Kafka and Anne Frank and Robert Burns, among others.

Ms. Rait has never been here, and she wants to come
here, and I want people to show her Faulkner country and
Salinger country and to give her one heck of a good time.
It is easy to give her a good time. I watched her in ecstasy
about Paris last October. That was during one of the four

trips she has taken outside of her native country in her nearly seventy-five years. She showed me Versailles, which was a sensational novelty to both of us. "I make you a *present* of this," she said. Her English is excellent.

Her health is excellent too. So are her literary tastes. Translators in the U.S.S.R. discover what they think are good books in foreign languages, and then they have to persuade their Government to publish them. And when one considers the books which Rita Rait has caused to be read by her people, one is bound to admit that she has done as much for international understanding on a deep level as anybody around. I would be charmed to see this acknowledged in history books.

She has been around a long time, and has known a lot of famous people. She was a child before the Revolution. She took a degree in physiology under Pavlov. Think of that. She is the widow of a submarine commander, a man not especially enthusiastic about literature. She respected that lack of enthusiasm.

And when she gets here, if she gets here, it will be discovered that she is comparably unenthusiastic about, in fact strikingly ignorant of, economic and political affairs. Her passionate opinions on various Soviet writers, for example, have nothing to do with whether they are in political favor or not. All she cares about is whether or not they can write for sour apples.

She is easy to embarrass, as are a lot of people, and I was pleased to embarrass her about piracy of books as practiced so smarmily in the U.S.S.R. The scheme is this: Foreigners' books are published there without permission from their authors. This has happened to several of my books, and I haven't even been notified of their publication. The smarmy part is that royalties based on God-only-knows-what are deposited to each author's credit just as secretly in accounts God-only-knows-where. The rumor is that an author can spend that money only in the U.S.S.R. This much is sure: It can't be given to Solzhenitsyn. Graham Greene tried to do that years ago—and fizzled, of course.

Other socialist countries make more honorable and open deals. And I told Rita Rait that only Formosa treated foreign writers as insultingly as the U.S.S.R. This shriveled her. "Only Formosa," she echoed. "I will tell them," she said. I expect she did, too. She hadn't been afraid to tell them to publish Kafka, so she couldn't have hesitated to tell them that.

And Russia will no doubt improve its copyright manners by and by. We can wait, I suppose. But while we are waiting, we should demonstrate our own good manners by inviting Rita Rait to have a look at us before she is too old to travel anymore. There is paperwork to do. As I understand it, important universities should ask her to come on solemn, scholarly business. Our own Department of State must also indicate its pleasure with the prospect of such a distinguished guest. I am seeking the proper authorities, who know how these things are done. I would be enchanted if the proper authorities would in turn get in touch with me.

Be warned: She isn't absolutely crazy about Dostoevsky. Neither does she think Solzhenitsyn's new novel is as good as a lot of foreigners seem to think it is. His earlier novels have convinced her, though, that the U.S.S.R. should be proud of him as a writer. How is she as a translator? I've been told she's first-rate by those who are entitled to an opinion. Her *Catcher in the Rye* is one of the sensational best sellers of all time over there. Like writers for *The Times,* she wasn't allowed to say "F--- you" but she is proud of finding an old Russian expression which was so quaint that it had no status as being officially obscene. Nobody complained about it, and the book was published as translated. Much to her satisfaction, the quaint expression in the context of Salinger's masterpiece was neither more nor less offensive than, in her opinion, Salinger would have wanted it to be.

Address to P.E.N. Conference in Stockholm, 1973

JOURNALISTS and teachers are often bullied or fired in my country—for saying this or that. But writers of novels and plays and short stories and poems have never been hurt or hampered much. They haven't even been noticed much by federal, state, or local governments, no matter how insolent or blasphemous or treasonous those writers may be. This has been going on now for nearly two hundred years.

If tyranny comes to my country, which is an old one now (and tyranny can come anywhere, anytime, as nearly as I can tell), I expect to go on writing whatever I please, without putting myself in danger, as long as what I write is fiction. The experience of American power structures with fiction since 1776 would appear to validate what is perhaps the first poem I ever learned by heart. A playmate must have taught it to me. It goes like this:

> *Sticks and stones*
> *May break my bones,*
> *But words can never hurt me.*

It is the feeling in several countries, I know, that fiction can hurt a social order a lot. And by fiction I mean any person's written report of what is going on in his head, as opposed to the daily news. Writers of such stuff, as Heinrich Böll can tell us, have been jailed, put into lunatic asylums, exiled, or even killed sometimes—for putting certain words in a certain order. Politicians who do things like that to fiction writers should learn from the American experience that they are not merely being cruel. They are being preposterous, too. Fiction is harmless. Fiction is so much hot air.

The Vietnam war has proved this. Virtually every American fiction writer was against our participation in that civil war. We all raised hell about the war for years and years—with novels and poems and plays and short stories. We dropped on our complacent society the literary equivalent of a hydrogen bomb.

I will now report to you the power of such a bomb. It has the explosive force of a very large banana-cream pie —a pie two meters in diameter, twenty centimeters thick, and dropped from a height of ten meters or more.

Address to P.E.N. Conference in Stockholm, 1973

My own feeling is that we should turn this awesome weapon over to the United Nations, or to some other international peacekeeping organization, such as the C.I.A.

What can tyrants, large and small, learn from my speech so far? That fiction writers are harmless. They may safely be allowed all the freedoms which birds have—to sing as they please, to hop about, to fly. Harsh authorities everywhere should learn this poem by heart, and recite it joyfully at the start of every day:

> *Sticks and stones*
> *May break my bones,*
> *But fiction can never hurt me.*

Thus ends the public part of my speech.

I have a few additional words for you, my colleagues. Please don't repeat them outside this room. While it is true that we American fiction writers failed to modify the course of the war, we have reason to suspect that we have poisoned the minds of thousands or perhaps millions of American young people. Our hope is that the poison will make them worse than useless in unjust wars.

We shall see.

Unfortunately, that still leaves plenty of Americans who don't read or think much—who will still be extremely useful in unjust wars. We are sick about that. We did the best we could.

Most writers I know, all over the world, do the best they can. They must. They have no choice in the matter. All artists are specialized cells in a single, huge organism, mankind. Those cells have to behave as they do, just as the cells in our hearts or our fingertips have to behave as they do.

We here are some of those specialized cells. Our purpose is to make mankind aware of itself, in all its complexity, and to dream its dreams. We have no choice in the matter.

And there is more to our situation than that. In privacy here, I think we can acknowledge to one another that we don't really write what we write. We don't write the *best* of what we write, at any rate. The best of our stuff draws information and energy and wholeness from outside ourselves. Sculptors feel this more strongly than we do, incidentally. Every sculptor I ever knew felt that some spook had taken possession of his hands.

Where do these external signals come from? I think they come from all the other specialized cells in the organism. Those other cells contribute to us energy and little bits of information, in order that we may increase the organism's awareness of itself—and dream its dreams.

But if the entire organism thinks that what we do is important, why aren't we more influential than we are? I am persuaded that we are tremendously influential, even though most national leaders, my own included, probably never heard of most of us here. Our influence is slow and subtle, and it is felt mainly by the young. They are hungry for myths which resonate with the mysteries of their own times.

We give them those myths.

We will become influential when those who have listened to our myths have become influential. Those who rule us now are living in accordance with myths created for them by writers when *they* were young. It is perfectly clear that our rulers do not question those myths for even a minute during busy day after busy day. Let us pray that those terribly influential writers who created those our leaders' were humane.

Thank you.

A
Political
Disease*

I WORRY about the
health of Dr. Hunter Thompson. I think I am supposed
to do that. He is the most creatively crazy and vulnerable
of the New Journalists, seemingly, and scattered throughout his dispatches are alarming reports on his health. Nor
are his sicknesses imaginary. In this, his latest book, he
gives the opinion of a physician: "He'd never seen anybody with as bad a case of anxiety as I had. He said I was
right on the verge of a complete mental, physical, and
emotional collapse."

Why would he tell us this? What could this be but a cry
for help? And what can we do to help him? It isn't as

*Review of Fear and Loathing: On the Campaign Trail '72, *by Dr. Hunter S.*
Thompson

231

though he doesn't try to help himself. He isn't like George Orwell, for instance, who is said to have been fairly listless in fighting disease. Thompson, if he is to be believed, has sampled the entire rainbow of legal and illegal drugs in heroic efforts to feel better than he does. He says in another book, *Fear and Loathing in Las Vegas,* that the trunk of his rented red Chevrolet convertible

> looked like a mobile police narcotics lab. We had two bags of grass, seventy-five pellets of mescaline, five sheets of high-powered blotter acid, a salt shaker half full of cocaine, and a whole galaxy of multi-colored uppers, downers, screamers, laughers . . . and also a quart of tequila, a quart of rum, a case of Budweiser, a pint of raw ether and two dozen amyls.

Again: What can we do to help him? I do not know him, except from his books, which are brilliant and honorable and valuable. The evidence in those argues that reality is killing him, because it is so ugly and cheap. He imagines in his new book that reality, and hence his health, might be improved if nobler men held office in this country and addressed themselves truthfully to the problems of our time. Here is what he wrote as he gathered strength to cover the most recent Presidential campaign:

> I have been through three Presidential elections now, but it has been twelve years since I could look at a ballot and see a name I wanted to vote *for.* . . . Now, with another one of these big bogus showdowns looming down on us, I can already pick up the stench of another bummer.

He covered the campaign for *Rolling Stone.* His night-mares were illustrated by Ralph Steadman, who has become as magically integral to Thompson's work as Sir John Tenniel was to *Through the Looking Glass* and *Alice in Wonderland*. And when the campaign was over, Thompson was more wretched than ever, concluding that McGovern was too ordinary a Democrat, too much a compromiser, to thrill the American people with dreams of greatness and rebirth and reform. The closing event for Thompson was the Super Bowl. He is a former sportswriter, like James Reston, whom he calls "the swinging Calvinist"; and his most effective metaphors have to do with athletic contests. Duane Thomas, the mute black unemployed fullback is, incidentally, Thompson's idea of a really splendid American citizen.

And when the Super Bowl was over, *and* the campaign, *and* the book about the campaign, Thompson made an impudent, mocking telephone call to Frank Mankiewicz, McGovern's most vibrant strategist. And then:

> I hung up and drank some more gin. Then I put a Dolly Parton album on the tape machine and watched the trees outside my balcony getting lashed around in the wind. Around midnight, when the rain stopped, I put on my special Miami Beach nightshirt and walked several blocks down La Cienega Boulevard to the Losers' Club.

There is plenty of news in this newest *Fear and Loathing* book. Thompson suggests, for instance, that the person who created the poisonous statement "I stand behind Tom Eagleton 1,000 percent" was not McGovern. It may have been Eagleton who did that, telling reporters what McGovern supposedly said. And Thompson detests Eagleton as much as he adores Duane Thomas. He calls the Senator "an opportunistic liar," "a hack," and "another one of those cheap hustlers," among other things.

Insults of that sort, isolated in a review, convey the idea of journalism at least as contemptible as the man attacked. But in the context of such a long and passionate book, such lapses seem almost beautiful. Curiously, they are so frenzied, so grotesque, that they can do no harm to Eagleton. I am extremely grateful for the New Journalism, as many responsible people are not. And what I think about it now is that it is the literary equivalent of Cubism: All rules are broken; we are shown pictures such as no mature, well-trained artist ever painted before, and in the crazy new pictures we somehow see luminous new aspects of beloved old truths.

I can put it more gruesomely—calling attention to the way people behave under torture sometimes, the way they are likely to thrash around and say things they might not say under other circumstances: The New Journalists are Populists screaming in pain.

They believe that it is easy and natural for Americans to be brotherly and just. That illusion, if it is an illusion, is the standard for well-being in the New Journalists' minds. Any deviation from that standard is perceived as a wound or a sickness. So the present atmosphere in America seems to them to be like the famous torture described by Orwell of tying the victim's hands and enclosing his head in a cage. And then a hungry rat is put into the cage.

I hasten to testify that the American atmosphere isn't *really* that terrifying. I am only saying that we have in our midst some people, like Hunter Thompson, who are supersensitive. Practically everybody else feels fine, just fine.

As for those who wish to know more about Thompson and his ideals, his frazzled nervous system, his self-destructiveness, and all that—he is unabridgeable. He is that rare sort of American author who must be read. He makes exciting, moving collages of carefully selected junk. They must be experienced. They can't be paraphrased.

As for the truth about his health: I have asked around about it. I am told that he appears to be strong and rosy, and steadily sane. But we will be doing what he wants us to do, I think, if we consider his exterior a sort of Dorian Gray facade. Inwardly, he is being eaten alive by tinhorn politicians.

The disease is fatal. There is no known cure. The most we can do for the poor devil, it seems to me, is to name his disease in his honor. From this moment on, let all those who feel that Americans can be as easily led to beauty as to ugliness, to truth as to public relations, to joy as to bitterness, be said to be suffering from Hunter Thompson's disease. I don't have it this morning. It comes and goes. This morning I don't have Hunter Thompson's disease.

Playboy Interview

PLAYBOY: Beyond the fact that it's become a profitable way to make a living, why do you write?

VONNEGUT: My motives are political. I agree with Stalin and Hitler and Mussolini that the writer should serve his society. I differ with dictators as to *how* writers should serve. Mainly, I think they should be—and biologically *have* to be—agents of change. For the better, we hope.

PLAYBOY: Biologically?

VONNEGUT: Writers are specialized cells in the social organism. They are evolutionary cells. Mankind is trying to become something else; it's experimenting with new ideas all the time. And writers are a means of introducing new ideas into the society, and also a means of responding symbolically to life. I don't think we're in control of what we do.

Kurt Vonnegut, Jr.

PLAYBOY: What *is* in control?

VONNEGUT: Mankind's wish to improve itself.

PLAYBOY: In a Darwinian sense?

VONNEGUT: I'm not very grateful for Darwin, although I suspect he was right. His ideas make people crueler. Darwinism says to them that people who get sick deserve to be sick, that people who are in trouble must deserve to be in trouble. When anybody dies, cruel Darwinists imagine we're obviously improving ourselves in some way. And any man who's on top is there because he's a superior animal. That's the social Darwinism of the last century, and it continues to boom. But forget Darwin. Writers are specialized cells doing whatever we do, and we're expressions of the entire society—just as the sensory cells on the surface of your body are in the service of your body as a whole. And when a society is in great danger, we're likely to sound the alarms. I have the canary-bird-in-the-coal-mine theory of the arts. You know, coal miners used to take birds down into the mines with them to detect gas before men got sick. The artists certainly did that in the case of Vietnam. They chirped and keeled over. But it made no difference whatsoever. Nobody important cared. But I continue to think that artists—all artists—should be treasured as alarm systems.

PLAYBOY: And social planners?

VONNEGUT: I have many ideas as to how Americans could be happier and better cared for than they are.

PLAYBOY: In some of your books—especially *The Sirens of Titan* and *Slaughterhouse-Five*—there's a serious notion that all moments in time exist simultaneously, which implies that the future can't be changed by an act of will in the present. How does a desire to improve things fit with that?

VONNEGUT: You understand, of course, that everything I say is horseshit.

PLAYBOY: Of course.

VONNEGUT: Well, we do live our lives simultaneously. That's a *fact.* You *are* here as a child and as an old man. I recently visited a woman who has Hodgkin's disease. She has somewhere between a few months and a couple of years to live, and she told me that she was living her life simultaneously now, living *all* the moments of it.

PLAYBOY: It still seems paradoxical.

VONNEGUT: That's because what I've just said to you is horseshit. But it's a useful, comforting sort of horseshit, you see? That's what I object to about preachers. They don't say anything to make anybody any happier, when there are all these neat lies you can tell. And everything is a lie, because our brains are two-bit computers, and we can't get very high-grade truths out of them. But as far as improving the human condition goes, our minds are certainly up to that. That's what they were designed to do. And we do have the freedom to make up comforting lies. But we don't do enough of it. One of my favorite ministers was a guy named Bob Nicholson. He looked like Joseph Cotten, and he was a bachelor Episcopalian priest up on Cape Cod. Every time one of his parishioners died, he went all to pieces. He was outraged by death. So it was up to his congregation and the relatives of the deceased to patch him up, get him pumped up on Christianity sufficiently to get through the funeral service. I liked that very much: Nothing he was going to say in the standard Episcopalian funeral oration was going to satisfy *him*. He needed better lies.

PLAYBOY: Did you come up with any?

VONNEGUT: I tried. Everybody did. It was a very creative situation, with a minister of God falling apart like that.

PLAYBOY: What are some of the lies you like?

VONNEGUT: "Thou shalt not kill." That's a good lie. Whether God said it or not, it's still a perfectly good lie. And if it gives it more force to say that God said it, well, fine.

PLAYBOY: What's your religious background?

VONNEGUT: My ancestors, who came to the United States a little before the Civil War, were atheists. So I'm not rebelling against organized religion. I never had any. I learned my outrageous opinions about organized religion at my mother's knee. My family has always had those. They came here absolutely crazy about the United States Constitution and about the possibility of prosperity and the brotherhood of man here. They were willing to work very hard, and they were atheists.

PLAYBOY: Do you think organized religion can make anybody happier?

VONNEGUT: Oh, of course. Lots of comforting lies are told in church—not enough, but some. I wish preachers would lie more convincingly about how honest and brotherly we should be. I've never heard a sermon on the subject of gentleness or restraint; I've never heard a minister say it was wrong to kill. No preacher ever speaks out against cheating in business. There are fifty-two Sundays in a year, and somehow none of these subjects comes up.

PLAYBOY: Is there any religion you consider superior to any other?

VONNEGUT: Alcoholics Anonymous. Alcoholics Anonymous gives you an extended family that's very close to a blood brotherhood, because everybody has endured the same catastrophe. And one of the enchanting aspects of Alcoholics Anonymous is that many people join who *aren't* drunks, who pretend to be drunks because the social and spiritual benefits are so large. But they talk about real troubles, which aren't spoken about in church, as a rule. The halfway houses for people out of prisons, or for people recovering from drug habits, have the same problems: people hanging around who just want the companionship, the brotherhood or the sisterhood, who want the extended family.

PLAYBOY: Why?

VONNEGUT: It's a longing for community. This is a lonesome society that's been fragmented by the factory system. People have to move from here to there as jobs move, as prosperity leaves one area and appears somewhere else. People don't live in communities permanently anymore. But they should: Communities are very comforting to human beings. I was talking to a United Mine Workers lawyer in a bar down in the Village the other day, and he was telling me how some miners in Pennsylvania damn well will not leave, even though the jobs are vanishing, because of the church centered communities there, and particularly because of the music. They have choirs that are 100 years old, some of them, extraordinary choirs, and they're not going to leave that and go to San Diego, and build ships or airplanes. They're going to stay in Pennsylvania, because that's home. And that's intelligent. People should have homes. My father and grandfather were both architects—my grandfather was the first licensed architect in Indiana—and he built a home with the idea that it would be inhabited by several generations. Of course, the house is an undertaking parlor or a ukulele institute now. But during his lifetime, my father built two dream homes with the idea that further generations would live there. I would like there to be ancestral homes for all Americans somewhere.

PLAYBOY: But you're living in a New York apartment now.

VONNEGUT: Well, I'm used to the rootlessness that goes with my profession. But I would like people to be able to stay in one community for a lifetime, to travel away from it to see the world, but always to come home again. This is comforting. Whenever I go to Indianapolis now, a childish question nags at me, and I finally have to say it out loud: "Where is my bed?" I grew up there, and nearly 1,000,000 people live there now, but there is no place in that city where a bed is mine. So I ask, "Where is my bed?"—and then wind up in a Holiday Inn. You can't go home again.

Until recent times, you know, human beings usually had a permanent community of relatives. They had dozens of homes to go to. So when a married couple had a fight, one or the other could go to a house three doors down and stay with a close relative until he was feeling tender again. Or if a kid got so fed up with his parents that he couldn't stand it, he could march over to his uncle's for a while. And this is no longer possible. Each family is locked into its little box. The neighbors aren't relatives. There aren't other houses where people can go and be cared for. When Nixon is pondering what's happening to America—"Where have the old values gone?" and all that—the answer is perfectly simple. We're lonesome. We don't have enough friends or relatives anymore. And we would if we lived in real communities.

PLAYBOY: How do you feel about those who are making attempts at alternate social structures—such as communes?

VONNEGUT: They want to go back to the way human beings have lived for 1,000,000 years, which is intelligent. Unfortunately, these communities usually don't hold together very long, and finally they fail because their members aren't really relatives, don't have enough in common. For a community really to work, you shouldn't have to wonder what the person next to you is thinking. That is a primitive society. In the communities of strangers that are being hammered together now, as young people take over farms and try to live communally, the founders are sure to have hellish differences. But their children, if the communes hold together long enough to raise children, will be more comfortable together, will have more attitudes and experiences in common, will be more like genuine relatives.

PLAYBOY: Have you done any research on this?

VONNEGUT: No. I'm afraid to. I might find out it wasn't true. It's a sunny little dream I have of a happier mankind. I couldn't survive my own pessimism if I didn't have some kind of sunny little dream. That's mine, and don't tell me I'm wrong: Human beings *will* be happier —not when they cure cancer or get to Mars or eliminate racial prejudice or flush Lake Erie but when they find ways to inhabit primitive communities again. That's my utopia. That's what I want for me.

PLAYBOY: You don't have a community?

VONNEGUT: Oh, there are a lot of people who'll talk to me on the telephone. And I always receive nice welcomes at Holiday Inns, Quality Motor Courts, Ramada Inns.

PLAYBOY: But you have no relatives?

VONNEGUT: Shoals of them, but scattered to hell and gone, and thinking all kinds of crazy different ways.

PLAYBOY: You want to be with people who live nearby and think exactly as you do?

VONNEGUT: No. That isn't primitive enough. I want to be with people who don't think at all, so I won't have to think, either. I'm very tired of thinking. It doesn't seem to help very much. The human brain is too high-powered to have many practical uses in this particular universe, in my opinion. I'd like to live with alligators, think like an alligator.

PLAYBOY: Could this feeling come from the fatigue of having just finished a book?

VONNEGUT: No.

PLAYBOY: Even though you'd rather be an alligator, could we talk about people some more?

VONNEGUT: People are too good for this world.

PLAYBOY: You must have seen or heard of human communities that you'd like to join.

VONNEGUT: Artists of different kinds constitute a sort of extended family. I'm already in that, I guess. Artists usually understand one another fairly well, without anybody's having to explain much. There's one commune I admire here in New York, but I wouldn't want to join it. It was founded by a woman I know. It's based on everybody's screwing everybody else. This is intelligent, because it makes sort of a blood tie. It's actually a jism tie, but anything of a magical nature like that really does tend to make a person more of a relative. It's taken her a long time to construct this, because there are a lot of people who can never relate that way, who can't get through the barriers. But it's like the brotherhood ceremony in *Tom Sawyer,* when Tom and Huck sign oaths in their own blood. Vital substances are involved. I saw a thing on television recently about the exploration of the upper Nile; the British expedition was stopped by one of the tribal chiefs, and the chief wouldn't let them go on until they mingled their blood with the chief's blood. Another New York woman I know has a commune based on eating big bowls of chili or spaghetti or rice every night. Those are also vital substances.

PLAYBOY: This longing for community may explain, at least in part, the Jesus-freak movement among young people. But why do you think they're attracted to fundamentalist Christianity?

VONNEGUT: Well, the choice of a core for an artificial extended family is fairly arbitrary. I've already mentioned the arts and jism and blood and spaghetti. Christianity is equally commonplace and harmless, and therefore good. Do you know what nucleation is? I don't, but I'll pretend I do. It has to do with how big something has to be in order to grow rather than die out. The standard example is starting a fire in a coal furnace. If the fire you start is below a certain size, it will go out. If it's larger than that, it will spread until all the fuel is on fire. Clumps of cancer cells are probably forming in us all the time and petering out—because the clumps are below a certain size. In America, it's easy to form a large clump of people who know something about Christianity, since there has always been so much talk about Christianity around. It wouldn't be easy to get a large clump of Zoroastrians, for instance.

245

But there are very big clumps of Christianity. There are very big clumps of race hatred. It's easy to make either one of them grow, especially in a society as lonesome as this one is. All kinds of clumps.

PLAYBOY: So you don't admire Christianity any more or less than, say, a communal bowl of spaghetti every evening? Or anything else that might hold an extended family together?

VONNEGUT: I admire Christianity more than anything— Christianity as symbolized by gentle people sharing a common bowl.

PLAYBOY: You speak of gentle people, but somehow all this talk of Jesus freaks and extended families brings Charles Manson to mind.

VONNEGUT: Yes, it does. His, of course, was an extended family. He recruited all these dim-witted girls, homeless girls, usually—girls who felt homeless, at any rate—and the family meant so much to them that they would do anything for it. They were simple and they were awfully young.

PLAYBOY: What do you think Manson's appeal was to them?

VONNEGUT: His willingness to be father. It's one of the weaknesses of our society that so few people are willing to be father, to be responsible, to be the organizer, to say what's to be done next. Very few people are up to this. So if somebody is willing to take charge, he is very likely to get followers—more than he knows what to do with. The standard behavior pattern in our society now is for the father to deny he's father as soon as he possibly can, when the kid is sixteen or so. I assume that Charles Manson projected not only a willingness to become father but to remain father and become grandfather and then great-grandfather. There was a permanence there that people haven't been able to get from their own parents.

PLAYBOY: And if father happens to be evil, you just take your chances.

VONNEGUT: Sure. What the hell? You just got born and you're going to leave before you know it.

PLAYBOY: Do you have any suggestions on how to put together healthier extended families than Manson's?

VONNEGUT: Sure. Put Christianity or spaghetti instead of murder at their core. I recommend this for countries, too.

PLAYBOY: Is there some way our country could encourage the growth of extended families?

VONNEGUT: By law. I'm writing a Kilgore Trout story about that right now.

PLAYBOY: Kilgore Trout is the fictitious science-fiction writer you've used in some of your novels.

VONNEGUT: That's true. And he's writing a story now about a time when our Government understands that it isn't taking care of the people because it's too clumsy and slow. It wants to help people, but it can't get anywhere in time. So the President happens to visit Nigeria, where extended families have been the style since the beginning of time. He is impressed, and properly so. Huge families take care of their own sick and old, of any relative in trouble. They do it right away and at no cost to the Government. So the President of the United States comes home and he announces that the trouble with the country is that nobody has enough relatives within shouting distance. Nobody can just yell for help. Everybody has to fill out forms. So the President is going to have the computers of the Social Security Administration assign everybody thousands of relatives.

PLAYBOY: At random?

VONNEGUT: Higgledy-piggledy. You have to throw out whatever middle name you have and substitute whatever name the computers give you—names of Greek gods, colors, chemical elements, flowers, animals. The story begins with a political refugee coming to America, and he not only has to swear allegiance to the country and all that, he also has to accept a new middle name from the computers. They give him the middle name Daffodil. His name becomes Laszlo Daffodil Blintz. He has 20,000 relatives all over the country with the same Government Issue middle name. He gets a Daffodil family directory, a subscription to the Daffodil family's monthly magazine. There would be lots of ads in there for jobs, things to buy, things to sell.

PLAYBOY: Wouldn't his GI relatives take advantage of him?

VONNEGUT: If they asked for too much, he could tell them to go screw, just the way he would a blood relative. And there would be ads and articles in the family monthly about crooks or deadbeats in the family. The joy of it would be that nobody would feel alone and anybody who needed seven dollars until next Tuesday or a baby-sitter for an hour or a trip to the hospital could get it. Whenever I'm alone in a motel in a big city, I look up Vonneguts and Liebers in the telephone book, and there never are any. Lieber was my mother's maiden name. But if I were a Daffodil or a Chipmunk or a Chromium, there would be plenty of numbers to call.

PLAYBOY: What if they didn't want to hear from you?

VONNEGUT: That's a fairly standard experience with relatives. It's also fairly standard for relatives to be *glad* to hear from you, to help if they can.

PLAYBOY: They wouldn't be compelled by law to give you what you wanted?

VONNEGUT: Hell, no. It would be like regular relatives, only there would be slews of them. If some guy came ringing my doorbell and he said, "Hey, you're a Chipmunk and I'm a Chipmunk; I need a hundred dollars," I would listen to his story, if I felt like it, and give him what I could spare, what I thought he deserved. It could be zero. And it wouldn't turn the country into a sappy, mawkish society, either. There would be more people telling each other to go screw than there are right now. A panhandler could come up to you and say, "Hey, buddy, can you help a fella out?" And you could ask him his middle name, and he might say, "Chromium," and you could say, "Screw you. I'm a Chipmunk. Go ask a Chromium for help."

Eventually, of course, the Chromiums would start thinking they were just a little bit better than the Daffodils and "I don't know what it is about those Chipmunks," and so on, but there would also be people of all backgrounds meeting as relatives. "Are you an Emerald? Shit, I'm an Emerald, too! Where are you from?" I know that as far as Vonneguts go, I've got some claim on those people. I got a postcard on my fiftieth birthday signed by a lot of people named Vonnegut—a Catholic branch around Oakland, California. I don't know how they found out it was my birthday, but I got this marvelous card and I'd never met them.

One time a few years ago, I was speaking at the University of Hawaii and somebody came up to me and said, "Who's Fred Vonnegut?" I said I didn't know and he told me that Fred Vonnegut's name was in the newspaper all the time. So I picked up a Honolulu paper and in it there was this big used-car ad with a picture of Fred and a headline like "COME IN AND ASK FRED VONNEGUT FOR A GOOD DEAL." So I looked him up and we had supper together. Turned out that he grew up in Samoa and his mother was a Finn. But the meeting, the connection, was exciting to both of us.

PLAYBOY: Aren't links by name, though, what you call a false *karass* in *Cat's Cradle*—a group that finds its identity in an irrelevant or artificial shared experience?

VONNEGUT: I don't know, but if it works, it doesn't matter. It's like the drug thing among young people. The fact that they use drugs gives them a community. If you become a user of any drug, you can pick up a set of friends you'll see day after day, because of the urgency of getting drugs all the time. And you'll get a community where you might not ordinarily have one. Built around the marijuana thing was a community, and the same is true about the long-hair thing: You're able to greet and trust strangers because they look like you, because they use marijuana, and so forth. These are all magical amulets by which they recognize one another —and so you've got a community. The drug thing is interesting, too, because it shows that, damn it, people are wonderfully resourceful.

PLAYBOY: How so?

VONNEGUT: Well, thousands of people in our society found out they were too stupid or too unattractive or too ignorant to rise. They realized they couldn't get a nice car or a nice house or a good job. Not everybody can do that, you know. You must be very pleasant. You must be good-looking. You must be well connected. And they realized that if you lose, if you don't rise in our society, you're going to live in the midst of great ugliness, that the police are going to try to drive you back there every time you try to leave. And so people trapped like that have really considered all the possibilities. Should I paint my room? If I get a lot of rat poison, will the rats go away? Well, no. The rats will still be there, and even if you paint it, the room will still be ugly. You still won't have enough money to go to a movie theater; you still won't be able to make friends you like or can trust.

So what can you do? You can change your *mind.* You can change your insides. The drug thing was a perfectly marvelous, resourceful, brave experiment. No government would have dared perform this experiment. It's the sort of thing a Nazi doctor might have tried in a concentration camp. Loading everybody in block C up with amphetamines. In block D, giving them all heroin. Keeping everyone in block E high on marijuana—and just seeing what happened to them. But this experiment was and continues to be performed by volunteers, and so we know an awful lot now about how we can be changed internally. It may be that the population will become so dense that *everybody*'s going to live in ugliness, and that the intelligent human solution—the only possible solution—will be to change our insides.

PLAYBOY: Have drugs been a solution for you?

VONNEGUT: No—although I did get into the prescribed-amphetamines thing because I was sleeping a lot. I've always been able to sleep well, but after eight hours of sleep, I'd find myself taking a nap in the afternoon. I found I could sleep from one to five if I wanted to, spend the afternoon seeing wonderful color movies. It's a common response to depression. I was taking these enormous naps and I decided it was a waste of time. So I talked to a doctor about it and she prescribed Ritalin. It worked. It really impressed me. I wasn't taking a whole lot of it, but it puzzled me so much that I could be depressed and just by taking this damn little thing about the size of a pinhead, I would feel much better. I used to think that I was responding to Attica or to the mining of the harbor of Haiphong. But I wasn't. I was obviously responding to internal chemistry. All I had to do was take one of those little pills. I've stopped, but I was so interested that my mood could be changed by a pill.

PLAYBOY: Do you experience manic periods as well as depressive ones?

VONNEGUT: Until recently, about every twenty days, I blew my cork. I thought for a long time that I had perfectly good reasons for these periodic blowups; I thought people around me had it coming to them. But only recently have I realized that this has been happening regularly since I've been six years old. There wasn't much the people around me could do about it. They could probably throw me off a day or so, but it was really a pretty steady schedule.

PLAYBOY: You say *was.*

VONNEGUT: Well, I've been taking lessons in how to deal with it. I've been going to a doctor once a week. It isn't psychoanalysis: It's a more superficial sort of thing. I'm talking to her about depression, trying to understand its nature. And an awful lot of it is physiological. In this book I've just finished, *Breakfast of Champions,* the motives of all the characters are explained in terms of body chemistry. You know, we don't give a shit about the characters' childhoods or about what happened yesterday—we just want to know what the state of their bloodstreams is. They're up when their bloodstreams are up and they're down when their bloodstreams are down. But for me, this year is a much better one than last year was. Depressions really had me, and they don't this year. I'm managing much better. I was really very down the last couple of years, and by working at it, I've gotten myself up again. I'm getting help from intelligent people who aren't Freudians.

PLAYBOY: Early on in *Slaughterhouse-Five,* you mention getting a little drunk at night and calling old friends long distance. Do you still do that?

VONNEGUT: Not anymore. But it's wonderful. You can find anybody you want in the whole country. I love to muck around in the past, as long as there are real people and not ghosts to muck around with. I knew an obstetrician who was very poor when he was young. He went to California and he became rich and famous. He was an obstetrician for movie stars. When he retired, he went back to the Midwest and looked up all the women he'd taken out when he was nobody. He wanted them to see he was somebody now. "Good for you," I said. I thought it was a charming thing to do. I like people who never forget.

I did a crazy thing like that myself. At Shortridge High School, when I went there, we had a senior dance at which comical prizes were given to different people in the class. And the football coach—he was a hell of a good coach, we had a dynamite football team—was giving out the presents. Other people had rigged them, but he was passing them out, announcing what the present was for each person. At that time, I was a real skinny, narrow-shouldered boy.

PLAYBOY: Like Billy Pilgrim in *Slaughterhouse?*

VONNEGUT: Right. I was a preposterous kind of flamingo. And the present the coach gave me was a Charles Atlas course. And it made me sick. I considered going out and slashing the coach's tires, I thought it was such an irresponsible thing for an adult to do to a kid. But I just walked out of the dance and went home. The humiliation was something I never forgot. And one night last year, I got on the phone and called Indianapolis information and asked for the number of the coach. I got him on the phone and told him who I was. And then I reminded him about the present and said, "I want you to know that my body turned out all right." It was a *neat* unburdening. It certainly beats psychiatry.

PLAYBOY: In your books, a real sadness darkens all the fun. Despite your apparently successful self-therapy, do you consider yourself basically sad?

VONNEGUT: Well, there are sad things from my childhood, which I assume have something to do with my sadness. But any sadness I feel now grows out of frustration, because I think there is so much we can do—things that are cheap—that we're not doing. It has to do with ideas. I'm an atheist, as I said, and not into funerals—I don't like the idea of them very much—but I finally decided to go visit the graves of my parents. And so I did. There are two stones out there in Indianapolis, and I looked at those two stones side by side and I just wished—I could hear it in my head, I knew so much what I wished—that they had been happier than they were. It would have been so goddamned easy for them to be happier than they were. So that makes me sad. I'm grateful that I learned from them that organized religion is anti-Christian and that racial prejudices are stupid and cruel. I'm grateful, too, that they were good at making jokes. But I also learned a bone-deep sadness from them. Kids will learn anything, you know. Their heads are empty when they're born. Grown-ups can put anything in there.

PLAYBOY: Why were your parents so sad?

VONNEGUT: I can guess. I can guess that the planet they loved and thought they understood was destroyed in the First World War. Something I said earlier, that human beings were too good for this planet; that was probably the sadness in their bones. That's hogwash, of course. They wrecked their lives thinking the wrong things. And, damn it, it wouldn't have taken much effort to get them to think about the right things.

PLAYBOY: Are you like your character Eliot Rosewater in the sense of feeling very tender about all the sadness in the world?

VONNEGUT: It's sort of self-congratulatory to be the person who walks around pitying other people. I don't do that very much. I just know that there are plenty of people who are in terrible trouble and can't get out. And so I'm impatient with those who think that it's easy for people to get out of trouble. I think there are some people who really need a lot of help. I worry about stupid people, dumb people. Somebody has to take care of them, because they can't hack it. One thing I tried to get going at one time was a nonprofit organization called Life Engineering. If you didn't know what to do next and you came to us, we'd *tell* you. Our only requirement would be that you had to do what we told you. You'd have to absolutely promise to do whatever

Kurt Vonnegut, Jr.

we'd say, and then we'd give you the best possible answer we could. But it turned out that nobody ever kept his promise and we had no way of enforcing it. We couldn't bring in a couple of hit men from Detroit.

PLAYBOY: Another way of dealing with sadness, of coming to terms with problems you can't solve, is through humor. Is that your way?

VONNEGUT: Well, I try. But laughter is a response to frustration, just as tears are, and it solves nothing, just as tears solve nothing. Laughing or crying is what a human being does when there's nothing else he can do. Freud has written very soundly on humor—which is interesting, because he was essentially such a humorless man. The example he gives is of the dog who can't get through a gate to bite a person or fight another dog. So he digs dirt. It doesn't solve anything, but he has to do *something.* Crying or laughing is what a human being does instead. I used to make speeches a lot, because I needed the money. Sometimes I was funny. And my peak funniness came when I was at Notre Dame, at a literary festival there. It was in a huge auditorium and the audience was so tightly tuned that everything I said was funny. All I had to do was cough or clear my throat and the whole place would break up. This is a really horrible story I'm telling. People were laughing because they were in agony, full of pain they couldn't do anything about. They were sick and helpless because Martin Luther King had been shot two days before. The festival had been called off on the Thursday he was shot, and then it was resumed the next day. But it was a day of grieving, of people trying to pull themselves together. And then, on Saturday, it was my turn to speak. I've got mildly comical stuff I do, but it was in the presence of

grief that the laughter was the greatest. There was an
enormous need to either laugh or cry as the only possible adjustment. There was nothing you could do to
bring King back. So the biggest laughs are based on the
biggest disappointments and the biggest fears.

PLAYBOY: Is that what's called black humor? Or is *all*
humor black?

VONNEGUT: In a sense, it probably is. Certainly, the people Bruce Jay Friedman named as black humorists
weren't really very much like one another. I'm not a
whole lot like J. P. Donleavy, say, but Friedman saw
some similarity there and said we were both black
humorists. So critics picked up the term because it was
handy. All they had to do was say black humorists and
they'd be naming twenty writers. It was a form of short-
hand. But Freud had already written about gallows
humor, which is middle-European humor. It's people
laughing in the middle of political helplessness. Gallows
humor had to do with people in the Austro-Hungarian
Empire. There were Jews, Serbs, Croats—all these
small groups jammed together into a very unlikely sort
of empire. And dreadful things happened to them. They
were powerless, helpless people, and so they made jokes.
It was all they could do in the face of frustration. The
gallows humor that Freud identifies is what we regard
as Jewish humor here: It's humor about weak, intelligent people in hopeless situations. And I have customarily written about powerless people who felt there
wasn't much they could do about their situations.

One of my favorite cartoons—I think it was by Shel
Silverstein—shows a couple of guys chained to an eigh-
teen-foot cell wall, hung by their wrists, and their ankles
are chained, too. Above them is a tiny barred window

that a mouse couldn't crawl through. And one of the guys is saying to the other, "Now here's my plan. . . ." It goes against the American storytelling grain to have someone in a situation he can't get out of, but I think this is very usual in life. There are people, particularly dumb people, who are in terrible trouble and never get out of it, because they're not intelligent enough. And it strikes me as gruesome and comical that in our culture we have an expectation that a man can always solve his problems. There is that implication that if you just have a little more energy, a little more fight, the problem can always be solved. This is so untrue that it makes me want to cry—or laugh. Culturally, American men aren't supposed to cry. So I don't cry much—but I do laugh a lot. When I think about a stupid, uneducated black junkie in this city, and then I run into some optimist who feels that any man can lift himself above his origins if he's any good—that's something to cry about or laugh about. A sort of braying, donkeylike laugh. But every laugh counts, because every laugh *feels* like a laugh.

PLAYBOY: What sort of things strike you as genuinely funny?

VONNEGUT: Nothing really breaks me up. I'm in the business of making jokes; it's a minor art form. I've had some natural talent for it. It's like building a mousetrap. You build the trap, you cock it, you trip it, and then bang! My books are essentially mosaics made up of a whole bunch of tiny little chips; and each chip is a joke. They may be five lines long or eleven lines long. If I were writing tragically, I could have great sea changes there, a great serious steady flow. Instead, I've gotten into the joke business. One reason I write so slowly is that I try to make each joke work. You really have to or the books are lost. But joking is so much a part of my life adjustment that I would begin to work on a story on any subject and I'd find funny things in it or I would stop.

PLAYBOY: How did you happen to begin writing?

VONNEGUT: The high school I went to had a daily paper, and has had since about 1900. They had a printing course for the people who weren't going on to college, and they realized, "My goodness, we've got the linotypes—we could easily get out a paper." So they started getting out a paper every day, called the *Shortridge Echo.* It was so old my parents had worked on it. And so, rather than writing for a teacher, which is what most people do, writing for an audience of one—for Miss Green or Mr. Watson—I started out writing for a large audience. And if I did a lousy job, I caught a lot of shit in twenty-four hours. It just turned out that I could write better than a lot of other people. Each person has something he can do easily and can't imagine why everybody else is having so much trouble doing it. In my case, it was writing. In my brother's case, it was mathematics and physics. In my sister's case, it was drawing and sculpting.

PLAYBOY: Were you already into science fiction by then?

VONNEGUT: Most of it was in the pulps, you know. I would read science-fiction pulps now and then, the same way I'd read sex pulps or airplane pulps or murder pulps. The majority of my contemporaries who are science-fiction writers now went absolutely bananas over science-fiction pulps when they were kids, spending all their money on them, collecting them, trading them, gloating over them, cheering on authors the straight world thought were hacks. I never did that, and

I'm sorry. I'm shy around other science-fiction writers, because they want to talk about thousands of stories I never read. I didn't think the pulps were beneath me; I was just pissing away my life in other ways.

PLAYBOY: Such as?

VONNEGUT: I dunno. I used to say I wasted eight years building model airplanes and jerking off, but it was a little more complicated than that. I read science fiction, but it was conservative stuff—H. G. Wells and Robert Louis Stevenson, who's easily forgotten, but he wrote *Jekyll and Hyde.* And I read George Bernard Shaw, who does an awful lot of extrapolating, particularly·in his introductions. *Back to Methuselah* was science fiction enough for me.

PLAYBOY: What do you think of it as a form? The standard critical appraisal is that it's low rent.

VONNEGUT: Well, the rate of payment has always been very low compared with that for other forms of writing. And the people who set the tone for it were the pulp writers. There's an interesting thing: When IBM brought out an electric typewriter, they didn't know if they had a product or not. They really couldn't imagine that anybody was *that* discontented with the typewriter already. You know, the mechanical typewriter was a wonderful thing; I never heard of anybody's hands getting tired using one. So IBM was worried when they brought out electric typewriters, because they didn't know whether anybody would have any use for them. But the first sales were made to pulp writers, writers who wanted to go faster because they got paid so much a word. But they were going so fast that characterization didn't matter and dialog was wooden and all that

—because it was always first draft. That's what you sold, because you couldn't afford to take the time to sharpen up the scenes. And so that persisted, and young people deciding to become science-fiction writers would use as models what was already being written. The quality was usually terrible, but in a way it was liberating, because you were able to put an awful lot of keen ideas into circulation fast.

PLAYBOY: What attracted you to using the form yourself?

VONNEGUT: I was working for General Electric at the time, right after World War Two, and I saw a milling machine for cutting the rotors on jet engines, gas turbines. This was a very expensive thing for a machinist to do, to cut what is essentially one of those Brancusi forms. So they had a computer-operated milling machine built to cut the blades, and I was fascinated by that. This was in 1949 and the guys who were working on it were foreseeing all sorts of machines being run by little boxes and punched cards. *Player Piano* was my response to the implications of having everything run by little boxes. The idea of doing that, you know, made sense, perfect sense. To have a little clicking box make all the decisions wasn't a vicious thing to do. But it was too bad for the human beings who got their dignity from their jobs.

PLAYBOY: So science fiction seemed like the best way to write about your thoughts on the subject?

VONNEGUT: There was no avoiding it, since the General Electric Company *was* science fiction. I cheerfully ripped off the plot of *Brave New World,* whose plot had been cheerfully ripped off from Eugene Zamiatin's *We.*

PLAYBOY: Slaughterhouse-Five is mainly about the Dresden fire bombing, which you went through during World War Two. What made you decide to write it in a science-fiction mode?

VONNEGUT: These things are intuitive. There's never any strategy meeting about what you're going to do; you just come to work every day. And the science-fiction passages in *Slaughterhouse-Five* are just like the clowns in Shakespeare. When Shakespeare figured the audience had had enough of the heavy stuff, he'd let up a little, bring on a clown or a foolish innkeeper or something like that, before he'd become serious again. And trips to other planets, science fiction of an obviously kidding sort, is equivalent to bringing on the clowns every so often to lighten things up.

PLAYBOY: While you were writing *Slaughterhouse-Five,* did you try at all to deal with the subject on a purely realistic level?

VONNEGUT: I couldn't, because the book was largely a found object. It was what was in my head, and I was able to get it out, but one of the characteristics about this object was that there was a complete blank where the bombing of Dresden took place, because I don't remember. And I looked up several of my war buddies and they didn't remember, either. They didn't want to talk about it. There was a complete forgetting of what it was like. There were all kinds of information surrounding the event, but as far as my memory bank was concerned, the center had been pulled right out of the story. There was nothing up there to be recovered—or in the heads of my friends, either.

PLAYBOY: Even if you don't remember it, did the experience of being interned—and bombed—in Dresden change you in any way?

VONNEGUT: No. I suppose you'd think so, because that's the cliché. The importance of Dresden in my life has been considerably exaggerated because my book about it became a best seller. If the book hadn't been a best seller, it would seem like a very minor experience in my life. And I don't think people's lives are changed by short-term events like that. Dresden was astonishing, but experiences can be astonishing without changing you. It did make me feel sort of like I'd paid my dues —being as hungry as I was for as long as I was in prison camp. Hunger is a normal experience for a human being, but not for a middle-class American human being. I was phenomenally hungry for about six months. There wasn't nearly enough to eat—and this is sensational from my point of view, because I would never have had this experience otherwise. Other people get hit by taxicabs or have a lung collapse or something like that, and it's impressive. But only being hungry for a while—my weight was 175 when I went into the Army and 134 when I got out of the P.O.W. camp, so we really were hungry—just leads to smugness now. I stood it. But one of my kids, at about the same age I was, got tuberculosis in the Peace Corps and had to lie still in a hospital ward for a year. And the only people who get tuberculosis in our society now are old people, skid-row people. So he had to lie there as a young man for a year, motionless, surrounded by old alcoholics—and this *did* change him. It gave him something to meditate about.

PLAYBOY: What did your experience in Dresden give *you* to meditate about?

VONNEGUT: My closest friend is Bernard V. O'Hare—he's a lawyer in Pennsylvania, and he's in the book—I asked him what the experience of Dresden meant to him and he said he no longer believed what his Government said. Our generation did believe what its Government said— because we weren't lied to very much. One reason we weren't lied to was that there wasn't a war going on in our childhood, and so essentially we were told the truth. There was no reason for our Government to lie very elaborately to us. But a government at war does become a lying government for many reasons. One reason is to confuse the enemy. When we went into the war, we felt our Government was a respecter of life, careful about not injuring civilians and that sort of thing. Well, Dresden had no tactical value; it was a city of civilians. Yet the Allies bombed it until it burned and melted. And then they lied about it. All that was startling to us. But it doesn't startle anybody now. What startled everybody about the carpet bombing of Hanoi wasn't the bombing; it was that it took place at Christmas. That's what everybody was outraged about.

PLAYBOY: As an ex-prisoner of war, how do you feel about the P.O.W.s returning from Vietnam?

VONNEGUT: Well, they were obviously primed to speak as they did by our own Government. But that shouldn't surprise us. In any case, these men have blatantly vested interests: They were highly paid technicians in this war. Our 45,000 white crosses in Vietnam were the children of lower-class families. The casualties have been hideous in the coal fields of Pennsylvania and in the ghettos. These people didn't make a lot of money out of the war, don't have lifetime careers. War was hell for them, and these highly paid executives are coming back saying, "Yes, it's a wonderful business." They get paid as much, some of them, as the managing editor of a big magazine gets paid. They're professional warriors who'll go anywhere and fight anytime.

PLAYBOY: You don't seem particularly sympathetic about their internment.

VONNEGUT: I'm pigheaded about certain things. I'm pigheaded about the difference between the Air Force and the Infantry. I like the Infantry. If there were another war, and if I were young enough, and if it were a just war, I'd be in the Infantry again. I wouldn't want to be in anything else. Before the Calley thing, I thought that infantrymen were fundamentally honorable—and there was that feeling among infantrymen of other countries at war, too. That much about war was respectable and the rest was questionable—even the artillery, you know, hiding in the woods and lobbing shells. That's foolish, but I still feel it. Also, I hate officers.

PLAYBOY: Why?

VONNEGUT: They're all shits. Every officer I ever knew was a shit. I spoke at West Point on this subject and they found it very funny. But all my life I've hated officers, because they speak so badly to the ground troops. The way they speak to lower-ranking persons is utterly unnecessary. A friend of mine was here the other day and he had bought a new overcoat he was very proud of. But I didn't like it, because it had epaulets—and I think he's going to take them off.

PLAYBOY: Judging from *Player Piano,* which is a strong indictment of scientists and the scientific way of looking at the world, you don't overly love *them,* either. In the twenty-one years since the book was published, has your attitude toward them changed?

VONNEGUT: Well, *scientists* have changed considerably.

It turns out that people will follow stereotypes because it makes things easier for everybody else. It used to be that professors really *were* absentminded; it was expected of them and they could get away with it. So they would cultivate it until it became a habit—missing appointments, forgetting important anniversaries—but they don't do that anymore. And it used to be that scientists were often like Irving Langmuir. He was a Nobel Prize winner, and my brother, who is a fine scientist, worked with him—that's how I knew him. And he was childlike in social relationships and claimed that he was simply unearthing truth, that the truth could never hurt human beings and that he wasn't interested in the applications of whatever he turned up. Many scientists were that way—and I've known a hell of a lot of them, because at General Electric, I was a PR man largely for the research laboratory there. They had hundreds of first-class scientists. So I got to know them—low-temperature guys and crystallographers and electron microscopists and all those guys. I was there every day, sticking my nose in here and there and talking to them. And back then, around 1949, they were all innocent, all simply dealing with truth and not worried about what might be done with their discoveries.

PLAYBOY: The A-bomb had had no impact on their minds at that point?

VONNEGUT: No. But then they all woke up. They decided, "Goddamn it, we're going to start paying attention." So they *did,* and the Langmuir type of innocent no longer exists. It was a stereotype at one time and it was useful to the politicians and the industrialists that scientists wouldn't worry about the implications of their discoveries. But they've learned that anything they turn up will be applied if it can be. It's a law of life that if you turn up something that *can* be used violently, it *will* be used violently. I've been proud of my brother because of the actual innocence of his work—like cloud-seeding with dry ice and silver iodide. He discovered that silver iodide would make it snow and rain under certain conditions. And I watched his shock about a year ago when it came out that we had been seeding the hell out of Indochina for years. He had known nothing about it. It's something anybody can do. You and I, for instance, could start seeding right here in my backyard—all we'd need is some crummy smoke generator that would send up silver-iodide smoke. But my brother has always tried to be alert to the violent uses of what he might turn up, and it saddened him to find out that silver iodide had been used in warfare. So scientists *have* become concerned about the morality of what they're doing. It's been happening for some time. Several years ago, Norbert Wiener, the MIT mathematician, wrote in *Atlantic* that he wasn't going to give any more information to industry or the Government, because they weren't gentle people, because they don't have humane uses for things.

PLAYBOY: What about scientists such as Wernher Von Braun?

VONNEGUT: Well, he's an engineer, of course, not a scientist. But what do I think of him? I don't know him, but it seems to me that he has a heartless sort of innocence, the sort of innocence that would allow a man to invent and build an electric chair—as an act of good citizenship. He has been an inventor of weapons systems in the past. Inventors of weapons systems, and Leonardo da Vinci was among them, are not friends of the common man.

PLAYBOY: So far, at least, the space program has been a nonviolent application of science and technology. What are your feelings about it?

VONNEGUT: I went to the last moonshot; I had never seen one before. I've been against the space program, just because it was so expensive and because we were in such a terrible hurry to do it. We've had the technology for a while to do it, but it seems to me that there is certainly no rush about getting to the moon and spending so much money doing it. We might plan in the next 500 years to explore the moon. After all, we knew there were no resources we could economically bring back from there, and we knew there was no atmosphere. Even if the whole thing were paved with diamonds, that wouldn't help us much. So it seems like a vaudeville stunt. A lot of scientists felt it was money that might be spent in other areas of research. What it was, was money spent on engineering. It might as well have been an enormous skyscraper or a huge bridge or something like that. It was publicity and show business, not science. John F. Kennedy was largely responsible for it. He was competitive. He was a tough, joyful athlete and he loved to win. And it wasn't a bad guess, really, that this might cheer Americans up and make us more energetic. It didn't quite work out that way, but Kennedy, in his enthusiasm for this thing, was really wishing the best for the American people. He thought it might excite us tremendously.

PLAYBOY: When, in fact, most people got bored with it very quickly. Why do you think that happened?

VONNEGUT: It seemed childish. It seemed childish even to children. My children simply weren't interested. There was nothing they wanted on the moon. A third grader knows there's no atmosphere there. There's nothing to eat or drink, nobody to talk to. They already know that. There's more that they want in the Sahara or on the polar icecap.

PLAYBOY: The science-fiction versions of how it would happen were certainly more flamboyant than the actuality.

VONNEGUT: Well, they picked colorless men to make the trip, because colorless men were the only sort who could *stand* to make it. In science-fiction stories, people on spaceships are arguing all the time. Well, people who are going to argue shouldn't go on spaceships in the first place.

PLAYBOY: What was it like to be at the last shot?

VONNEGUT: It was a thunderingly beautiful experience— voluptuous, sexual, dangerous, and expensive as hell. Martha Raye was there. Don Rickles was there. Death was there.

PLAYBOY: Somebody died?

VONNEGUT: *Life* magazine died. They were down there with cameras that looked like siege howitzers. We hung around with them. We were down there on credentials from *Harper's*. When they got home with their pictures, they found out *Life* had died. How's that for a symbol? Our planet became *Life*less while our astronauts were on their way to the moon. We went down there because a Swedish journalist at a cocktail party in New York told us he cried at every launch. Also, my brother had told me, "When you see one go up, you almost think it's worth it."

Kurt Vonnegut, Jr.

PLAYBOY: You said it was sexual.

VONNEGUT: It's a tremendous space fuck, and there's some kind of conspiracy to suppress that fact. That's why all the stories about launches are so low-key. They never give a hint of what a visceral experience it is to watch a launch. How would the taxpayers feel if they found out they were buying orgasms for a few thousand freaks within a mile of the launch pad? And it's an extremely *satisfactory* orgasm. I mean, you *are* shaking and you *do* take leave of your senses. And there's something about the sound that comes shuddering across the water. I understand that there are certain frequencies with which you can make a person involuntarily *shit* with sound. So it does get you in the guts.

PLAYBOY: How long does that last?

VONNEGUT: Maybe a full minute. It was a night flight, so we were able to keep the thing in sight in a way that wouldn't have been possible in the daytime. So the sound seemed longer. But who knows? It's like describing an automobile accident; you can't trust your memory. The light was tremendous and left afterimages in your eyes; we probably shouldn't have looked at it.

PLAYBOY: How did the people around you react?

VONNEGUT: They were gaga. They were scrogging the universe. And they were sheepish and sort of smug afterward. You could see a message in their eyes, too: Nobody was to tell the outside world that NASA was running the goddamnedest massage parlor in history. When I got back to New York, I was talking to a cabdriver on the way in from the airport. He was talking about what I've always felt—that the money should be spent on space when we can *afford* it. He wanted better hospitals; he wanted better schools; he wanted a

270

house for himself. He was a very decent guy; he was no fool at all. He was working twenty-four hours a day—at the post office from two in the morning until three in the afternoon, and then he started driving his cab. And, believe me, he knew there was nothing on the moon. If NASA were to give him a trip to Cape Kennedy and a pass to the VIP section or the press section for the next launch, he'd find out where the real goodies are.

PLAYBOY: The Vietnam war has cost us even more than the space program. What do you think it's done to us?

VONNEGUT: It's broken our hearts. It prolonged something we started to do to ourselves at Hiroshima; it's simply a continuation of that: an awareness of how ruthless we are. And it's taken away the illusion that we have some control over our Government. I think we *have* lost control of our Government. Vietnam made it clear that the ordinary citizen had no way to approach his Government, not even by civil disobedience or by mass demonstration. The Government wasn't going to respond, no matter what the citizen did. That was a withering lesson. A while ago, I met Hans Morgenthau at a symposium at the United Nations and I was telling him that when I taught at Iowa and Harvard, the students could write beautifully but they had nothing to write about. Part of this is because we've learned over the past eight years that the Government will not respond to what we think and what we say. It simply is not interested. Quite possibly, the Government has *never* been interested, but it has never made it so clear before that our opinions don't matter. And Morgenthau was saying that he was about to start another book, but he was really wondering whether it was worth the trouble. If nobody's paying attention, why bother? It's a hell of a lot more fun to write a book that influences affairs in some way, that influences people's thinking. But the President has made it perfectly clear that he's insulated from such influences.

PLAYBOY: What's your opinion of Nixon?

VONNEGUT: Well, I don't think he's evil. But I think he dislikes the American people, and this depresses us. The President, particularly because of television, is in the position to be an extraordinarily effective teacher. I don't know exactly how much executive responsibility a President has, or how much the Government runs itself, but I do know that he can influence our behavior for good and ill. If he teaches us something tonight, we will behave according to that tomorrow. All he has to do is say it on television. If he tells us about our neighbors in trouble, if he tells us to treat them better tomorrow, why, we'll all try. But the lessons Nixon has taught us have been so mean. He's taught us to resent the poor for not solving their own problems. He's taught us to like prosperous people better than unprosperous people. He could make us so humane and optimistic with a single television appearance. He could teach us Confucianism.

PLAYBOY: Confucianism?

VONNEGUT: How to be polite to one another—no matter how angry or disappointed we may be—how to respect the old.

PLAYBOY: Humanity and optimism was the message that George McGovern was trying to get across. How do you account for his spectacular failure?

VONNEGUT: He failed as an actor. He couldn't create on camera a character we could love or hate. So America voted to have his show taken off the air. The American audience doesn't care about an actor's private life, doesn't want his show continued simply because he's honorable and truthful and has the best interests of the nation at heart in private life. Only one thing matters: Can he jazz us up on camera? This is a national tragedy, of course—that we've changed from a society to an audience. And poor McGovern did what any actor would have done with a failing show. He blamed the scripts, junked a lot of his old material, which was actually beautiful, called for new material, which was actually old material that other performers had had some luck with. He probably couldn't have won, though, even if he had been Clark Gable. His opponent had too powerful an issue: the terror and guilt and hatred white people feel for the descendants of victims of an unbelievable crime we committed not long ago— human slavery. How's that for science fiction? There was this modern country with a wonderful Constitution, and it kidnaped human beings and used them as machines. It stopped it after a while, but by then it had millions of descendants of those kidnaped people all over the country. What if they turned out to be so human that they wanted revenge of some kind? McGovern's opinion was that they should be treated like anybody else. It was the opinion of the white electorate that this was a dangerous thing to do.

PLAYBOY: If you had been the Democratic nominee, how would you have campaigned against Nixon?

VONNEGUT: I would have set the poor against the rich. I would have made the poor admit that they're poor. Archie Bunker has no sense of being poor, but he obviously is a frightened, poor man. I would convince Archie Bunker that he was poor and getting poorer, that the ruling class was robbing him and lying to him. I was invited to submit ideas to the McGovern campaign. Nothing was done with my suggestions. I wanted Sarge Shriver to say, "You're not happy, are you? Nobody in this country is happy but the rich people. Something is wrong. I'll tell you what's wrong: We're lonesome! We're being kept apart from our neighbors. Why? Because the rich people can go on taking our money away if we don't hang together. They can go on taking our power away. They *want* us lonesome; they want us huddled in our houses with just our wives and kids, watching television, because they can manipulate us then. They can make us buy anything, they can make us vote any way they want. How did Americans beat the Great Depression? We banded together. In those days, members of unions called each other 'brother' and 'sister,' and they meant it. We're going to bring that spirit back. Brother and sister! We're going to vote in George McGovern, and then we're going to get this country on the road again. We are going to band together with our neighbors to clean up our neighborhoods, to get the crooks out of the unions, to get the prices down in the meat markets. Here's a war cry for the American people: 'Lonesome no more!' " That's the kind of demagoguery I approve of.

PLAYBOY: Do you consider yourself a radical in any sense?

VONNEGUT: No, because everything I believe I was taught in junior civics during the Great Depression—at School 43 in Indianapolis, with full approval of the school board. School 43 wasn't a radical school. America was an idealistic, pacifistic nation at that time. I was taught in the sixth grade to be proud that we had a standing Army of just over a hundred thousand men and that the generals had nothing to say about what was done in Washington. I was taught to be proud of that and to pity Europe for having more than a million men under arms and spending all their money on airplanes and tanks. I simply never unlearned junior civics. I still believe in it. I got a very good grade.

PLAYBOY: A lot of young people share those values with you. Do you think that's the reason your books are so popular with them?

VONNEGUT: It could be something like that, but I truly don't know. I certainly didn't go after the youth market or anything like that. I didn't have my fingers on any pulse; I was simply writing. Maybe it's because I deal with sophomoric questions that full adults regard as settled. I talk about what is God like, what could He want, is there a heaven, and, if there is, what would it be like? This is what college sophomores are into; these are the questions they enjoy having discussed. And more mature people find these subjects very tiresome, as though they're settled.

PLAYBOY: Isn't that using "mature" ironically?

VONNEGUT: Not if you define mature as the way old people act, and immature as the way young people act.

PLAYBOY: But these questions remain important to you.

VONNEGUT: They're still entertaining to me. I'm not a vested interest, particularly. I don't want to find out what God wants so I can serve Him more efficiently. I don't want to find out what heaven is like so I can get ready for it. Thinking about those things makes me laugh after a while. I enjoy laughing, so I think about them and I laugh. I'm not sure why.

PLAYBOY: When did you start laughing about all this?

VONNEGUT: When I was just a little kid, I think. I'd wonder what life was all about, and I'd hear what grown-ups had to say about it, and I'd laugh. I've often thought there ought to be a manual to hand to little kids, telling them what kind of planet they're on, why they don't fall off it, how much time they've probably got here, how to avoid poison ivy, and so on. I tried to write one once. It was called *Welcome to Earth*. But I got stuck on explaining why we don't fall off the planet. Gravity is just a word. It doesn't explain anything. If I could get past gravity, I'd tell them how we reproduce, how long we've been here, apparently, and a little bit about evolution. And one thing I would really like to tell them about is cultural relativity. I didn't learn until I was in college about all the other cultures, and I should have learned that in the first grade. A first-grader should understand that his culture isn't a rational invention; that there are thousands of other cultures and they all work pretty well; that all cultures function on faith rather than truth; that there are lots of alternatives to our own society. I didn't find that out for sure until I was in the graduate school of the University of Chicago. It was terribly exciting. Of course, now cultural relativity is fashionable—and that probably has something to do with my popularity among young people. But it's more than fashionable—it's defensible, attractive. It's also a source of hope. It means we don't have to continue this way if we don't like it.

PLAYBOY: Whatever the reasons for your popularity, you've become genuinely famous in the past couple of years. Has that changed your life much?

VONNEGUT: The big problem is mail. I suppose I get about as much mail as Eddie Fisher does—about six letters a day. I get plenty of really thoughtful, charming letters. I keep meaning to answer them, but then I realize I'll never have a chance. So the stacks pile up—and they're all letters I mean to do something about. I had a secretary for a while; I thought I could use her to handle this enormous correspondence. But it turned out that it was taking half a day, every day, to dictate letters. Also, every time I answered a letter, I got a pen pal. So my mail increased geometrically.

PLAYBOY: Has popularity changed your life in any other way?

VONNEGUT: No. I'm just sorry it didn't happen sooner, because I was really very broke for a long time, when I had a lot of children. I could have bought neat vacations and wonderful playthings, and so forth. I mean, my children certainly had shoes, and some even had private educations, but I'm sorry the money wasn't spread out more evenly over the years. Now that they're all grown, the money has a slightly mocking quality. That's one of the things that's ridiculous about the economy as far as writers go. They get either $50 for something or $500,000—and there doesn't seem to be much in between.

PLAYBOY: Does your surge of popularity make you uncomfortable in any way?

VONNEGUT: No, it's all right, because it's the books that are popular. And I don't read them or think about them; they're just out in the world on their own. They aren't me. Neither is my reputation. I've pretty much stopped making public appearances, because I'm so unlike my books or my reputation. Strangers speak to me on the street in New York about three times a week. That cheers me up. I'm not crashingly famous and the

small fame I have came gradually. I admire Norman
Mailer very much—particularly his mental health—
because he absorbed the most terrific shock a mind can
absorb: to become famous at twenty-five. He held up
very well under the impact.

What's happened to me, though, is such a standard
American business story. As I said, my family's always
been in the arts, so the arts to me are business. I started
out with a pushcart and now I've got several supermar-
kets at important intersections. My career grew just the
way a well-managed business is supposed to grow. After
twenty years at a greasy grind, I find that all my books
are in print and selling steadily. They will go on selling
for a little while. Computers and printing presses are in
charge. That's the American way: If the machines can
find a way to use you, you will become a successful
businessman. I don't care much now whether the business grows or shrinks. My kids are grown. I have no
fancy uses for money. It isn't a love symbol to me.

PLAYBOY: What *is* a love symbol for you?

VONNEGUT: Fudge is one. An invitation to a cottage by
a lake is one.

PLAYBOY: Are you wealthy now?

VONNEGUT: I know a girl who is always asking people
that. I nearly drop my teeth every time she does it. My
mother told me that was practically the rudest question
a person could ask. The girl always gets an answer,
incidentally. The people give her a fairly clear idea of
their net worth. Then she asks where the money came
from and they tell her that, too. It sounds to me like
they're talking hard-core pornography. Anyway, my
wealth is mainly in the form of copyrights, which are
very valuable as long as the computers and the printing

presses think I'm their man. As for cash and real estate
and securities and all that, I'm nowhere near being a
millionaire, for instance. It doesn't now appear that I
will ever be one. The only way to get to be one is
through capital gains. I have nothing big coming up in
the way of capital gains. I'm a straight-income man.
And the hell with it. As I said, my children are all
grown now and it would wreck their heads if I started
rigging things so they could all be millionaires.

PLAYBOY: How does it feel to have been doing for years
what must have seemed to you like good work and only
now getting really noticed?

VONNEGUT: I don't feel cheated. I always had readers,
even when not much money was coming in. I was in
paperbacks, you see, and from the first, I was getting
friendly notes from strangers who had found me in PXs
and drugstores and bus stations. *Mother Night* and *Canary in a Cathouse* and *The Sirens of Titan* were all
paperback originals, and *Cat's Cradle* was written with
that market in mind. Holt decided to bring out a hardcover edition of *Cat's Cradle* after the paperback rights
had been sold. The thing was, I could get $3,000 im-
mediately for a paperback original, and I always needed
money right away, and no hardcover publisher would
let me have it.

But I was also noticing the big money and the heavy
praise some of my contemporaries were getting for their
books, and I would think, "Well, shit, I'm going to have
to study writing harder, because I think what I'm doing
is pretty good, too." I wasn't even getting reviewed.
Esquire published a list of the American literary world
back then and it guaranteed that every living author of
the slightest merit was on there somewhere. I wasn't on

there. Rust Hills put the thing together, and I got to know him later and I told him that the list had literally made me sick, that it had made me feel subhuman. He said it wasn't supposed to be taken seriously. "It was a joke," he said. And then he and his wife got out a huge anthology of high-quality American writing since World War Two and I wasn't in that, either.

Oh, well, what the hell. I was building a power base anyway, with sleazo paperbacks. This society is based on extortion, and you can have anything you want if you have a power base. The computers of my paperback publishers began to notice that some of my sleazo books were being reordered, were staying in print. So management decided to see what was in them. Hardcover publishers sniffed an opportunity. The rest is history—a Guggenheim, professorships, Elaine's. Allen Ginsberg and I both got elected to the National Institute of Arts and Letters this year and *Newsweek* asked me how I felt about two such freaks getting into such an august organization. I said, "If we aren't the establishment, I don't know who is."

PLAYBOY: Was *Slaughterhouse-Five* the first to sell well in hardcover?

VONNEGUT: Yes; it was an alternate selection for Literary Guild. And *Breakfast of Champions* is a primary selection for Literary Guild, Saturday Review Book Club and Book Find Club. But I'm sort of like Ted Williams now—I shuffle up to the plate. . . .

PLAYBOY: Do you think your writing will change much from now on?

VONNEGUT: Well, I felt after I finished *Slaughterhouse-Five* that I didn't have to write at all anymore if I didn't want to. It was the end of some sort of career. I don't know why, exactly. I suppose that flowers, when they're through blooming, have some sort of awareness of some purpose having been served. Flowers didn't ask to be flowers and I didn't ask to be me. At the end of *Slaughterhouse-Five,* I had the feeling that I had produced this blossom. So I had a shutting-off feeling, you know, that I had done what I was supposed to do and everything was OK. And that was the end of it. I could figure out my missions for myself after that.

PLAYBOY: Since *Breakfast of Champions* has just been published, you apparently decided to continue writing after *Slaughterhouse-Five.*

VONNEGUT: Well, *Slaughterhouse* and *Breakfast* used to be one book. But they just separated completely. It was like a pousse-café, like oil and water—they simply were not mixable. So I was able to decant *Slaughterhouse-Five,* and what was left was *Breakfast of Champions.*

PLAYBOY: What are you trying to say in *Breakfast?*

VONNEGUT: As I get older, I get more didactic. I say what I really think. I don't hide ideas like Easter eggs for people to find. Now, if I have an idea, when something becomes clear to me, I don't embed it in a novel; I simply write it in an essay as clearly as I can. What I say didactically in the introduction to *Breakfast of Champions* is that I can't live without a culture anymore, that I realize I don't have one. What passes for a culture in my head is really a bunch of commercials, and this is intolerable. It may be impossible to live without a culture.

PLAYBOY: Most of the people in *Breakfast* seem jangled and desperate—in situations they can't get out of—and a number of them consider suicide.

VONNEGUT: Yes, suicide is at the heart of the book. It's

also the punctuation mark at the end of many artistic careers. I pick up that punctuation mark and play with it in the book, come to understand it better, put it back on the shelf again but leave it in view. My fascination with it, the fascination of many people with it, may be a legacy from the Great Depression. That Depression has more to do with the American character than any war. People felt so useless for so long. The machines fired everybody. It was as though they had no interest in human beings anymore. So when I was a little kid, getting my empty head filled up with this and that, I saw and listened to thousands of people who couldn't follow their trades anymore, who couldn't feed their families. A hell of a lot of them didn't want to go on much longer. They wanted to die because they were so embarrassed. I think young people detect that dislike for life my generation often learned from our parents during the Great Depression. It gives them the creeps. Young people sense our envy, too—another thing we learned to do during the Thirties: to hunger for material junk, to envy people who had it. The big secret of our generation is that we don't like life much.

PLAYBOY: Do you think the younger generation likes it better than the previous two or three?

VONNEGUT: No, the younger generation probably doesn't like it, either. And some of the anger between the generations is the guilt and embarrassment of the parents at having passed this on. But the American experience has been an unhappy experience, generally, and part of it, as I say, is living without a culture. When you came over here on a boat or whatever, you abandoned your culture.

PLAYBOY: How has all this affected you personally?

VONNEGUT: All my books are my effort to answer that question and to make myself like life better than I do. I'm trying to throw out all the trashy merchandise adults put in my head when I was a little kid. I want to put a culture up there. People will believe anything, which means *I* will believe anything. I learned that in anthropology. I want to start believing in things that have shapeliness and harmony. *Breakfast of Champions* isn't a threat to commit suicide, incidentally. It's my promise that I'm beyond that now. Which is something for me. I used to think of it as a perfectly reasonable way to avoid delivering a lecture, to avoid a deadline, to not pay a bill, to not go to a cocktail party.

PLAYBOY: So your books have been therapy for yourself.

VONNEGUT: Sure. That's well known. Writers get a nice break in one way, at least: They can treat their mental illnesses every day. If I'm lucky, the books have amounted to more than that. I'd like to be a useful citizen, a specialized cell in the body politic. I have a feeling that *Breakfast* will be the last of the therapeutic books, which is probably too bad. Craziness makes for some beautiful accidents in art. At the end of *Breakfast,* I give characters I've used over and over again their freedom. I tell them I won't be needing them anymore. They can pursue their own destinies. I guess that means I'm free to pursue my destiny, too. I don't have to take care of them anymore.

PLAYBOY: Does that feel good?

VONNEGUT: It feels different. I'm always glad to feel something different. I've changed. Somebody told me the other day that that was the alchemists' secret: They weren't really trying to transmute metals. They only pretended to do that so they could have rich patrons.

What they really hoped to do was to change *themselves*.

PLAYBOY: What sort of things do you plan to write from now on?

VONNEGUT: I can guess. It isn't really up to me. I come to work every morning and I see what words come out of the typewriter. I feel like a copyboy whose job is to tear off stories from the teletype machine and deliver them to an editor. My guesses about what I'll write next are based on what has happened to other human beings as they've aged. My intuition will pooh out—my creative craziness; there will be fewer pretty accidents in my writing. I'll become more of an explainer and less of a shower. In order to have enough things to talk about, I may finally have to become more of an educated man. My career astonishes me. How could anybody have come this far with so little information, with such garbled ideas of what other writers have said? I've written enough. I won't stop writing, but it would be OK if I did.

One thing writing *Breakfast* did for me was to bring right to the surface my anger with my parents for not being happier than they were, as I mentioned earlier. I'm damned if I'll pass their useless sadness on to my children if I can possibly help it. In spite of chain-smoking Pall Malls since I was fourteen, I think my wind is still good enough for me to go chasing after happiness, something I've never really tried. I get more respect for Truman Capote as the years go by, probably because he's becoming genuinely wiser all the time. I saw him on television the other night, and he said most good artists were stupid about almost everything but their arts. Kevin McCarthy said nearly the same thing to me one time when I congratulated him for moving well in a play. He said, "Most actors are very clumsy offstage." I want to stop being stupid in real life. I want to stop being clumsy offstage.

Part of the trick for people my age, I'm certain, is to crawl out of the envying, life-hating mood of the Great Depression at last. Richard M. Nixon, who has also been unintelligent and unimaginative about happiness, is a child of the Great Depression, too. Maybe we can both crawl out of it in the next four years. I know this much: After I'm gone, I don't want my children to have to say about me what I have to say about my father: "He made wonderful jokes, but he was such an unhappy man."